The Religion of the Founding Fathers

David L. Holmes

Ash Lawn-Highland
The Clements Library

The Religion
of the
Founding Fathers

David L. Holmes
College of William and Mary

Ash Lawn-Highland:
The Home of James Monroe
and
The Clements Library,
University of Michigan

"The past is a foreign country; they do things differently there."

–L. P. Hartley

Acknowledgments

This small book allows me to thank the following graduates of the College of William and Mary who have assisted over the years in preparing this and other publications: Michael J. Lansing, Jennifer R. Loux, Daniel Vaca, and Kyle F. Zelner. Additional thanks go to Gillian R. Barr, Richard L. McCarty, Daniel Preston, David B. Voelkel, and the staffs of Ash Lawn-Highland and of The Clements Library. Kemper Conwell of Pixels in Charlottesville, Virginia, did a remarkable job in designing and preparing this manuscript for publication.

Library of Congress Cataloging-in-Publication Data

Holmes, David Lynn.
    The religion of the Founding Fathers / David L. Holmes.
        p. cm.
    Includes bibliographical references (p.) and index.
    1. Deism--United States. 2. Statesmen--Religious life--United
States--History--18th century. 3. United States--Religion--To 1800. I.
Title.

    BL2747.4.H65 2003
    200'.92'273--dc22

                                                    2003017599

Publication of this book by
Ash Lawn-Highland and
The Clements Library
is made possible by a generous donation
from alumni of the
College of William and Mary.

TABLE OF CONTENTS

FOREWORD

Many Americans believe they know the religious beliefs of the nation's Founding Fathers. More often than not, they are mistaken. Even today, knowing what people believe in their heart of hearts when we ask about their religious views is difficult. For most believers, there are days when "I BELIEVE!" accurately reflects their spirituality. On other occasions the indefinite answer "I believe?" is not only more honest but also much closer to the reality of the moment. Knowing what a public figure really believed more than two hundred years ago when the only connection with them is written documents— public announcements, fragments of private correspondence, the commentary of friends, clergy, relatives, newspaper editors, political opponents and two centuries of historical reflection—is a difficult task.

Still, far from lessening over time, the interest in the religious views of the Founding Fathers has increased over the past decades. Numerous books have appeared assigning the Founding Fathers to every religious category from atheism to Protestant evangelicalism. Clearly, Americans in the twenty-first century have many questions about the topic. Was Benjamin Franklin a Christian? Were any of the Founding Fathers? Did George Washington pray to God at Valley Forge? And if he did, does a prayer for deliverance from the horrors of war make him a lifetime evangelical? How did the youth or the schooling of the nation's Founders shape their beliefs? This lucid volume by David L. Holmes answers these questions and more.

As always, context, language, and understanding are key in any historical investigation. Thus Professor Holmes begins the compelling story of *The Religion of the Founding Fathers* with a survey of American religion in the late colonial period. In 1770, as he indicates, the religious climate in America was one of greater diversity than often imagined by today's citizenry. Many Americans are also unaware that the loudest cries for religious freedom and for the separation of civil and ecclesiastical authority came from the colonies with the strongest tradition of established churches, including Virginia and Massachusetts. The rich religious tapestry of the late colonial period provided the atmosphere in which the nation's Founders formed their beliefs.

Yet the question of how to relate the intensely private understanding of the religion of a figure such as Thomas Jefferson to the religious beliefs of the twenty-first century is complicated. The author's treatment of Jefferson's lifelong relationship with the church of his birth would be an enviable description of congregants for most twenty-first century clergy:

> *Jefferson was baptized, married, and buried under Anglican and Episcopal auspices. Raised on the prayers and psalms of the Book of Common Prayer, he could remember his mother teaching him prayers. Throughout life he remained outwardly an Episcopalian and committed the religious care of his children to that church. He regularly read the Bible.*

To identify Thomas Jefferson an Episcopalian, however, is problematic. His lifelong political opponents called Jefferson everything from an "atheist" to a "Deist" to a "Unitarian"—all terms that in their minds were indictments. But Jefferson often called himself a "Christian." Labels can be useful, but they can also be inaccurate. This is especially true when we classify people who, though dead for seven or eight generations, still live in our national psyche. It is especially problematic when we deal with a person as complex as Jefferson.

James Monroe's thoughts on religion have been an enigma to historians. Holmes's thorough analysis of Monroe, the most overlooked and understudied of the Founding Fathers, presents the first comprehensive study of his religion in modern historiography. In it we see Monroe, an intimate of the Deist icon Thomas Paine, as perhaps the most private and religiously skeptical of all of the Founders. Monroe's great passion, as Holmes points out, was for matters governmental, not spiritual—a focus that appears in his work, in his writings, and even in the eulogies delivered at his death.

In comparison to Monroe, the views of James Madison on religion are more available. One of the Rev. John Witherspoon's star students at Princeton, Madison spent an extra year at the college reading Hebrew. He could easily have followed the path of professional cleric. Instead, he became one of early America's champions of religious freedom. The author offers a surprise ending to his chapter on Madison by suggesting that the master of Montpelier may have ended his life as an evangelical Episcopalian.

What shouldn't be a surprise to any student of human nature is that religious views often change as long lives come close to an end. Certainly John Adams and Benjamin Franklin seemed to pay more attention to religion in their final years. In the final years leading to their mutually terminal Fourth of July, Adams and Jefferson frequently traded thoughts in their correspondence on this private subject. Written a few weeks before his death, Franklin's "Creed" comes as close to the comfort zone of belief of the average pew sitter in mainline American Christianity as one might reasonably determine, shy of firm belief in the divinity of Jesus Christ.

Trained in the fields of English, theology, and church history, Professor Holmes has focused his scholarly work—including a standard history of the Episcopal Church—on the development of American religion from the colonial period to the present. This well-written volume is a highly useful contribution to the historical literature dealing with the faith of the Founding Fathers. With the care and sensitivity of a seasoned historian, the author uses the available evidence to assure readers that the Founders of the republic, whose lives are chronicled herein, were indeed "sincere men of faith." At the end of the day, as at the end of time, this is what will have mattered.

John W. Turner
Religious Studies and Programs
The Colonial Williamsburg Foundation

1. RELIGION IN THE AMERICAN COLONIES IN 1770

"On my arrival in the United States," the famous French traveler Alexis de Tocqueville observed in the early nineteenth century "the religious aspect of the country was the first thing that struck my attention."[1] If in 1770—six years before the thirteen colonies became the United States—a different group of foreign visitors had traveled the narrow roads of the colonies, they would have agreed with de Tocqueville's later observance. The travelers would have further noted that the Americans of 1770 were either overwhelmingly Protestant or unchurched. Yet in such ports as Newport, R.I., New York City, Philadelphia,

Touro Synagogue, Newport, R.I.

Charleston, and Savannah—places where transatlantic vessels carrying passengers and crew regularly docked— the travelers would have come across not only Christian churches but also Jewish synagogues. As of 1770, some one thousand Jews probably lived in the colonies. In 1790, the first federal census counted 1,243 Jews in a total American population of almost three million.

In these and other port cities, the travelers would also have found scattered Roman Catholics. Most of the Roman Catholics lacked churches and priests, but some had "mass stations"—homes or buildings where itinerant priests said mass regularly or occasionally. The travelers would have found most of the approximately thirty thousand Roman Catholics and virtually all of their churches located in the colonies of Maryland and Pennsylvania, especially in polyglot Philadelphia.

When the Continental Congress was meeting, John Adams, George Washington, and others attended afternoon mass at St. Mary's Church, one of Philadelphia's two Roman Catholic Churches. The visit was apparently Adams's first to a Roman Catholic Church. The lavish ornamentation and use of Latin (a language the congregation did not understand) bothered the Puritan soul of Adams, but he also found the service appealing. "The dress of the priest was rich with lace," he wrote to his wife Abigail:

> His pulpit was velvet and gold. The altar piece was very rich—little images and crucifixes about—wax candles lighted up. But how shall I describe the picture of our Savior in a frame of marble over the altar

at full length Upon the Cross, in the
agonies, and the blood dropping and
streaming from his wounds?[2]

Both repelled and moved, Adams remained to the end of
the mass, describing the service to Abigail as "aw[e]ful
and affecting."[3]

A. The Sects

In 1770, the visitors would also have seen or heard
about a certain number of what in religious history are
often called "sects"—groups that remained within the
wide spectrum of Christian belief but that broke
off into what they considered pure communities of
ethics and doctrine based upon their interpretations
of Scripture.

And therein lies a story. From approximately the
fourth to the sixteenth century, certain practices or doctrines recorded in the New Testament or in the writings
of the early church fathers dropped out of use in
Christianity. The Protestant Reformation, beginning
with Martin Luther's ninety-five thesis of 1517, attempted to restore what it viewed as lost central teachings of
early Christianity. These teachings included the authority of Scripture, the lack of universal authority of the
Pope, the salvation of the individual by grace through
faith, the priesthood of all believers, the legitimacy of a
married clergy, the use of the vernacular (the language
commonly used in a country) for worship, and similar
doctrines. In the centuries prior to the Reformation, similar reform movements had broken out sporadically in

Europe, but none succeeded because the civil power, in union with the church, had put them down.

During and after the Reformation, however, new movements continually emerged in Christianity. Called by some church historians "the Radical Reformation," they attempted to restore more of the beliefs and rites of original Christianity than the mainline Protestant churches had thought necessary or appropriate. They restricted baptism to converted adults and separated church and state. Additionally, they refused, according to the teachings of Christ, to bear arms or to participate in war (a doctrinal practice called variously "non-resistance" or "pacifism"). These were three of their most radical reforms, though there were many others.

Other groups attempted to restore such practices as speaking in tongues during worship, the "love feast" (a common meal held by early Christians in connection with the Lord's Supper, or Holy Communion), the ritual of foot washing, the communalism depicted in the early chapters of the Book of Acts, the belief that Christ would soon return in majesty and power to judge the world, and other early Christian beliefs and practices. Persecuted in Europe, many of these groups immigrated to America during the colonial period. Following the Revolution and the subsequent separation of church and state, the United States became a fermenting vat of such Christian sects.

Thus while traveling through New England in 1770, the European visitors might have learned of the Sandemanians. Named for the leader who brought them from Scotland to New Hampshire, this small sect lived simply, opposed the accumulation of wealth, and observed a Lord's Supper that included a love feast and the ceremonial washing of feet. Other Sandemanian teachings—such as the dietary obligation of Christians to abstain not only from blood but also from the meat of animals killed by strangulation— returned the group to some of the practices of the earliest Jewish Christians.

Had the visitors traveled through New England one to two decades later, they would have learned of a growing movement of celibate, communal, pacifist Christians who worshiped uniquely and believed in the imminent Second Coming of Christ. Formally named the "United Society of Believers in Christ's Second Coming" and located in the state of New York as well as in New England, the sect was called by others "The Shakers." The travelers might also have encountered some members of the Universalist Church, a Christian group whose name came from their belief in universal salvation. Because God is merciful, Universalists believed, God would ultimately save all humans, not simply save some and consign all others to damnation. Their reading both of the New Testament and of early Christian history also caused them to question the Trinity, a doctrine officially defined by church councils beginning in the fourth century.

But the principal "sect" the travelers would have encountered would have been the Quakers, or the Religious Society of Friends. Plain in appearance, believing in an Inner Light that was the presence of Christ within each person, asserting the fundamental equality of all men and women, and opposing not only trained clergy and formal worship but also military service and the swearing of oaths, the Quakers were widely dispersed. Ranking as perhaps the fifth largest of the colonial churches, they existed in substantial numbers in Rhode Island, New York, New Jersey, Maryland, Virginia, North Carolina, and especially in Pennsylvania, a colony founded under Quaker auspices.

B. Tolerant Pennsylvania

Pennsylvania, in fact, would have been the colony in which the travelers would have encountered the richest mosaic of sects. Because the English Quaker William Penn had founded the colony as a "Holy Experiment" where Quakers and other persecuted religious sects could live and worship freely, Pennsylvania had attracted many small religious groups by 1770. The visitors would have discovered that most of the groups had come from Germany, that all believed that they had restored practices of apostolic Christianity that mainstream Christianity had wrongly abandoned, and that virtually all were pacifistic. Because of the pacifistic views of these sects, Pennsylvania was the only colony which did not have a legally instituted militia system, a situation the citizens had to rectify during the American Revolution.

Inland from Philadelphia, for example, the visitors would have encountered the *Unitas Fratrum*, or Moravian Brethren. Originating prior to the Protestant Reformation from the teachings of the Czech reformer John Huss, the Moravians refocused their teachings after they fled to the German state of Saxony in the eighteenth century. Valuing Christian conduct over the finer points of creeds, they were influenced both by Lutheran and Calvinist teachings. They stressed the inner testimony of the spirit and held to the principle of "in essentials unity; in non-essentials liberty; in both, charity." They celebrated a simple liturgy—or set of forms for public religious worship—marked by the rich use of music, attempted to reproduce the love feasts of early Christianity, and emphasized evangelism at a time when most Protestant churches did not. Pacifists, the Moravians were found not only in Pennsylvania but also in North Carolina and, briefly, in Georgia and elsewhere. In North Carolina they established the town of Salem; in Pennsylvania they settled Bethlehem, Nazareth, and Lititz. All of these towns were initially exclusively Moravian.

In counties adjacent to Philadelphia, the visitors might also have encountered a small mystical sect historically related to the Moravians. Named after a former follower who came to view Luther as a religious compromiser and called him "Dr. Sit-on-the-fence," the loosely organized, pacifistic, and somewhat mystical Schwenkfelders opposed infant baptism and emphasized inward spirituality over the doctrinal and churchly aspects of Christianity. Though residents of Pennsylvania for some decades by 1770, they had erected neither a meeting house nor a church building.

In colonial Pennsylvania, the visitors would also have encountered the Mennonites, the principal heirs of the radical Anabaptist (or "Rebaptizer") wing of the

Reformation. The program of the Mennonites to reproduce biblical Christianity caused them not only to deviate markedly from the norms of contemporary Christian orthodoxy of their day but also to suffer persecution. Rather than baptize infants, the Mennonites baptized only converted, believing adults. Rather than regard baptism as a sacrament that washed away original sin, they viewed it as a symbolic act that ratified an inner change that had already occurred in the converted individual. Instead of viewing Christianity as a religion into which people were born, they taught that churches should be "gathered" out of the world and composed of believing, converted adults who had voluntarily chosen to follow Jesus Christ.

Unlike Eastern Orthodoxy, Roman Catholicism, and such mainline Protestant movements as Lutheranism, Calvinism, and Anglicanism, the Mennonites and all Anabaptists advocated the separation of church and state. Teaching that the true Christian withdrew from the fallen world and rejected its values and amusements, they opposed wearing fashionable clothes, holding public office, using the courts, swearing oaths, and serving in the military. They took the doctrine of the priesthood of all believers so seriously that they selected their leaders by the biblical pattern of drawing lots. Whatever the visitors in 1770 would have thought of the Mennonites, the typical European of the time would have viewed them as akin to gypsies. Executed in Europe by Protestant and Roman Catholic countries alike for their teachings, the Mennonites lived and worshiped openly in tolerant Pennsylvania.

If the visitors had traveled inland to the mountainous areas of Pennsylvania and then down into the valleys of Maryland and Virginia, they would have encountered another group of "plain people" from Germany. Calling themselves by the biblical name of "Brethren" but referred to by others as "Dunkers" or "Tunkers" (from the German verb *tunken*, meaning "to dip"), the Brethren fully immersed (or "dunked") their adult baptizees in water three times face forward, once at the mention of each name of the Trinity. Heeding the instructions given in chapter five of the New Testament letter of James ("Is any among you sick? Let him call for the elders of the church, and let them pray over him, anointing him with oil in the name of the Lord."), they anointed the sick with oil. Basing their practice on the New Testament's depiction of the Last Supper, they held their solemn communion service in the evening and accompanied it with footwashing, a love feast, and the "holy kiss" (or kiss of charity) enjoined in the New Testament as a Christian greeting. Like many of the other Pennsylvania sects, they refused to swear oaths, bring civil suits in the courts, or bear arms.

The Ephrata Community of Lancaster County—a strict semi-monastic society noted for its choral music, printing, and illuminated manuscripts— represented a break-off from the Brethren. Besides adopting communal living, the Ephrata Community restored the early Christian practice of commemorating Saturday as the Sabbath. Although the community was in decline by 1770, the foreign travelers might have stopped there, for Ephrata was known for its hospitality and worship. At

A solitary sister at Ephrata cloister, depicted in 1745

least two of the Founding Fathers—Benjamin Franklin, who printed music books for the community and kept copies in his library, and George Washington, who used the Ephrata buildings as a temporary hospital for his wounded after the Battle of Brandywine—were well acquainted with the community.

In their attempt to return to first-century Christianity, all of these interpretations of Christianity differed markedly from those advocated by the mainstream of Christianity. But in colonial Pennsylvania, the Christian sects and the mainstream churches lived side by side. The European visitors would have chanced upon some sects and visited or heard about others, not only in Pennsylvania but also in other colonies. And in the years in which the affairs of the new nation centered in Philadelphia, the Founding Fathers of the United States would have encountered members of many of these sects.

C. The Mainline Churches

In 1770, sects were only footnotes to the story of religion in America. In that year the story focused on what were called "established churches" or "state churches." A concept transplanted to the American colonies from Europe, an established or state church is the official religious organization of a country or colony. The government supports it financially, legislates for it, and protects it against competition. Russia, Greece, Scandinavia, Germany, Italy, France, Spain, the Netherlands, England, Scotland, and other European countries all had state churches at one time. Citizens were born into membership in churches just as they were born into citizenship in countries. From the fourth century on, state churches represented the norm in European Christianity. Some European countries, such as England, still have them. Of the thirteen colonies that came to form the United States, nine had established churches during the colonial period.

RELIGION IN NEW ENGLAND

As the travelers worked their way down the colonies from north to south, they would have found one tolerant, religiously diverse colony in New England—Rhode Island. Founded by Roger Williams, an exile from Puritan Massachusetts who opposed governmental coercion in religious matters, the "livelie experiment" of Rhode Island had no established church. It guaranteed freedom of belief to all but outspoken atheists and—for some decades—to Roman Catholics. In the words of a critic from adjacent Massachusetts, the colony contained "Antinomians, Anabaptists, Antisabbatarians, Arminians, Socinians, Quakers, Ranters—everything in the world but Roman Catholics and real Christians."[4]

In this diverse colony, the Baptists (English Calvinists whose reading of the New Testament caused them to reject infant baptism and to baptize only believing adults), Quakers, Anglicans, and Congregationalists had the most members. Before he left the ministry and became a "Seeker" after a true Christianity that he never found, Williams had briefly been a Baptist.

By "real Christians," the Puritan critic of course meant his own Congregationalist Church, which was the established church not only in Massachusetts but also in Connecticut and New Hampshire. The largest of four branches of Calvinist Christianity the visitors would have observed in the colonies, Congregationalism arguably emphasized the intellect to a greater extent than any other church in colonial America. In the same way that other groups received their names from certain

First Baptist Church, Providence, R.I.,
where Brown University still holds commencements

acts (for example, the Quakers or Baptists) or modes of church governance (for example, the Presbyterians or Episcopalians), the Congregational churches took their name from the belief that early Christian congregations ran their own affairs and were subject to no higher supervision except that of Christ.

Congregationalism originated in the movement of English Calvinists called "Puritans"—a name acquired because of the efforts of its adherents to "purify" the Church of England from certain doctrines and liturgical practices that remained from its Roman Catholic past and were held to be untrue to the New Testament and to early Christian practice. The Puritan movement—both in the British Isles and in the American colonies—included the Presbyterians, the Baptists, and some Anglicans who decided to remain within England's established church.

In the backcountry of New England and especially in the colonies below it, the travelers would have encountered a third form of Calvinism—Presbyterianism (the name that Calvinism adopted in Scotland). In the area of Boston and especially in the colonies from New York to South Carolina, they would have learned of the Reformed (the name that Calvinism took on the European continent).

Except in two areas, these four groups shared the common heritage of Calvinism and displayed only minor homegrown dissimilarities in terminology and worship. Their principal differences lay in the areas of governance and baptismal practice. In matters of church government (or polity), the Congregationalists and Baptists followed a democratic form. The Presbyterians and

Reformed, however (like John Calvin himself), saw the republican form with an ascending hierarchy of synods and assemblies as true to the New Testament and to early Christianity. In matters of baptism, the Baptists believed that early Christians baptized only converted adults, whereas the Congregationalists, Presbyterians, and Reformed believed that the baptism of infants was true to apostolic practice.

Since all four Calvinist traditions gave laypeople significant authority in the government of the churches they insisted on an educated laity. As a result, these churches tended to found colleges wherever they went. As of 1770, two-thirds of the institutions of higher education in the American colonies were of Calvinist origin. Five years later, when Presbyterians founded a final college on the eve of the Revolution, the percentage of American colleges with a Congregationalist, Baptist, Presbyterian, or Reformed origin rose to seventy percent.

Church historians have estimated that over eighty percent of American Christians in the colonial period—from Anglicans on the right-center of the Christian spectrum to Quakers on the left—were significantly influenced by John Calvin's teachings. Only the Roman Catholics, some of the Lutherans, and some of the "sects" remained distinctly free from Calvinist influence. Even the Quakers—on the surface a very unCalvinistic body—were in reality the "puritans of the Puritans" and emerged in England from the left wing of the Puritan movement.

An interpretation of Christianity that professed less warmth and intimacy with God than Lutheranism or

Roman Catholicism, Calvinism was full of awe and homage to what it considered a just and majestic God. Like virtually all of Protestantism, it agreed with the main points of the Lutheran Reformation, but it viewed the Bible as more of a instruction manual for worship, church government, and conduct than Lutheranism did. Roman Catholicism, for example, taught that bishops were descendants of the apostles and were essential to the Christian faith. Luther held that early Christianity displayed a variety of forms of ordained ministry and that true Christianity could exist with or without bishops.

Calvin, however, believed that the New Testament (in such passages as Acts 20:17, 28 and Titus 1:5-7) indicated that bishops and presbyters—or, to use synonyms for the second word, "elders" or "priests"— were originally the same office. In Calvin's view, the separate office of a monarchical bishop (a bishop superior to all presbyters in rank and authority, in the same way that monarchs are superior to all of their subjects) emerged in Christianity only after the apostolic period. Thus Calvin argued that the presbyter-bishops who ministered in his churches—that is, the pastors— were just as much Christian bishops as the Pope of Rome, the Patriarch of Constantinople, or the Archbishop of Canterbury.

The key concept of Calvinism, that God is sovereign in all things, led to its teaching (a standard concept of the Protestant Reformation) that salvation comes entirely from God. Puritans believed that all humans were sinners through Adam's and Eve's Original Sin in the Garden of Eden, which was then transmitted to their descendants. Puritan doctrine asserted that humans could do nothing (in belief or in action) to save themselves, but that God out of his mercy did save some humans (the "elect") while damning others (the "reprobate"). Known as double predestination (the foreordination of individuals not only to heaven but also to hell), the doctrine was modified and ultimately abandoned in later centuries by the main bodies of Calvinism. John Calvin, however, asserted that the doctrine was taught in both the Old and New Testaments. It protected, he declared, the freedom of the all-knowing, all-powerful God.[5] He also observed that the doctrine was taught by many of the early church fathers, especially by Augustine of Hippo, the fourth-century bishop whose thought formed the basis of western Christian theology.

At its apex the doctrine had a great hold on believers. Its teachings are embedded in the familiar hymn, "Rock of Ages," written by an English Calvinist in 1776, six years after the foreign visitors would have toured the American colonies:

> Rock of ages, cleft for me,
> Let me hide myself in thee.
> Let the water and the blood
> From thy wounded side that flowed,
> Be of sin the double cure,
> Cleanse me from its guilt and power.
>
> Should my tears for ever flow,
> Should my zeal no langour know;
> All for sin could not atone:

Thou must save, and thou alone.
In my hand no price I bring,
Simply to thy cross I cling.

Three years later, another English Calvinist wrote what has perhaps become the best known hymn in the English language. Its words display not only the sovereignty of an all-powerful God but also the gratitude that predestinarian Calvinists have felt that God's grace might still save them despite all of their sin:

Through many dangers, toils, and snares,
I have already come.
T'is Grace that brought me safe thus far,
and Grace will lead me home.[6]

That both authors were clergy in the Church of England displays the widespread influence of Calvinism during the formative years of the United States. Anglicanism fused the influences of several Christian traditions and was not, strictly speaking, a Calvinist body. But churches, like political parties, have wings, and the Church of England contained a Calvinist wing.

As the visitors would have observed in New England, Puritans believed in the union of church and state. The teaching emerged from the Calvinist concern that every aspect of life should acknowledge God's sovereignty. In addition, it stemmed from the belief of Calvinists that God worked with humanity, as God had with the Israelites, through solemn agreements, or covenants. Only through the union of church and state,

Puritans believed, could humans produce a Christian society conformed to Scriptural teaching. Thus the Puritan colonies in New England were strict and intolerant on matters of doctrine and behavior, for their goal was to produce a sober, righteous, and godly Christian society. Although continually challenged by adversaries, the Puritan establishments were strong enough to survive into the early nineteenth century, longer than any other American state churches.

Readers can gain a good indication of where religious groups were concentrated in colonial America

Yale College and Chapel

by looking at its colleges. Since religious groups established all but one of the ten institutions of higher education in the colonies, the schools tended to be located where a denomination had strength.[7] Thus in New England, Harvard, Yale, and Dartmouth were Congregationalist, though Harvard later became Unitarian (a denomination that emerged from the liberal wing of Congregationalism). In Rhode Island, where several churches had strength, Baptists founded the College of Rhode Island (now Brown University). Since colonial colleges were small, there were probably fewer than one thousand college students in America at any time. The colleges had the primary purposes of producing ministers and educated laity for their denominations, though in time all accepted members of other churches. Although most student bodies were composed of young men from nearby areas, Brown enrolled Baptists from all over the colonies. Because of its reputation for Christian orthodoxy, Princeton attracted a steady stream of students from outside the middle colonies.

RELIGION IN THE MIDDLE COLONIES

In their travels through New England, the foreign visitors would have seen Anglican churches, for the Church of England began to grow significantly in Connecticut, Massachusetts, and Rhode Island during the eighteenth century. Although the Puritans had previously packed off to England or to more congenial colonies any residents who openly followed Anglican usages, they were obligated (as English citizens) to tolerate Anglicanism after the passage in 1689 of the English Toleration Act. Upon entering the most northern of the middle colonies, New York, the visitors would have learned that the only college in the colony—King's College (now Columbia University)—was an Anglican institution. Its existence testified to the status of the Church of England as the colony's established church, though only in the area of densest population from Staten Island to Westchester County.

Late arrivals in New York, the English seized the colony of New Netherland in 1664 from the original Dutch settlers. Changing its name and its language, they also changed the established church from Dutch Reformed to Anglican. Traces of the original Dutch presence remained not only in such names as "Harlem," "Bronx," "Brooklyn," and "Catskill" but also in the numbers of Reformed churches dotting the length of the Hudson River to Albany and beyond.

Always a minority faith in a colony whose diversity of nationality and religion rivaled that of Pennsylvania, Anglicanism nevertheless attracted many of the most influential families in New York. The principal organization for spreading Anglicanism in New York and elsewhere in the colonies was the London-based Society for the Propagation of the Gospel in Foreign Parts (S.P.G.), which sent more than three hundred missionaries to America through the end of the Revolutionary War. Not only Anglicans and Dutch Reformed but also Lutherans, Presbyterians, and Quakers maintained a significant presence in the colony. In addition, small numbers of Congregationalists, Mennonites, Jews, Roman Catholics, and other religious groups were in the colony from the seventeenth century on. French Reformed (or "Huguenots") fleeing persecution founded two French-speaking communities—New Paltz and New Rochelle—along the Hudson River. Settled in the 1600s first by the Dutch and then by the Swedes and Finns, New Jersey—like New York— subsequently became an English colony. In the late seventeenth century, Quakers, an affluent and significant presence in the colony, owned a part of it. Thus New Jersey, like Rhode Island, developed into a kind of religious free market. Scattered throughout the colony the foreign visitors would have found Baptist, Lutheran, Anglican, and a substantial number of Dutch Reformed, Quaker, and Presbyterian churches. The latter stemmed from the large numbers of Scots and Scots-Irish (Scots Presbyterians originally sent by the English crown across the Irish Sea to colonize and Protestantize Ireland in the 1600s) who chose to settle in New Jersey.

Along the Delaware River in both New Jersey and Pennsylvania, the visitors would have encountered the Lutheran remnants of Sweden's brief attempt in the seventeenth century to establish a New Sweden in America. The eight "Old Swedes" churches developed close relations with the Church of England and became Episcopalian after the Revolution. In New Jersey, Anglicanism grew slowly but steadily after the colony came under the control of the crown in 1702. The Anglican presence was significant enough to produce an unsuccessful plan to settle a bishop in Burlington, but the legislature, dominated by Quakers and by other dissenters, withstood all efforts to establish the Church of England. The colony's two colleges mirrored New Jersey's heterogeneity. The Dutch Reformed founded Queens College (now Rutgers University); Presbyterians established the College of New Jersey (now Princeton University).

In Pennsylvania the visitors would have come into contact not only with sects (as earlier described) but also with the mainstream Protestant churches. John Adams once wrote that Philadelphia included "Roman Catholics, English Episcopalians, Scotch and American Presbyterians, Methodists, Moravians, Anabaptists, German Lutherans, German Calvinists, Universalists, Arians, Priestleyans, Socinians, Independents, Congregationalists, . . . Deists and Atheists, and 'Protestants quie ne croyent rien.'"[8] So many Germans of Lutheran and Reformed (as well as sectarian) background settled in the fertile farmland of southeastern Pennsylvania that Benjamin Franklin reported the colony's population to be one-third German at the time of the Revolution. Scots-Irish Presbyterians emigrated to Pennsylvania in larger numbers than to any other colony, often squatting on land they did not own. Settling in the valleys in the mountainous central areas, they pushed westward towards Pittsburgh and southward via the Shenandoah Valley.

The foreign travelers would have found Philadelphia to be the metropolis of the thirteen colonies. The second largest city in the British empire by 1770, Penn's "City of Brotherly Love" served as an administrative center both for the Presbyterians and for the Baptists. It also contained the largest concentration of Jews in the colonies. Encompassing not only the congregations established in Pennsylvania by English and Welsh Baptists but also Baptist churches stretching from New England to Virginia, the Philadelphia Baptist Association sent out missionaries to gather new congregations. To produce a ministry for them, it founded the College of Rhode Island, in the colony where Baptists had possessed major strength. By 1770, however, the colonies of Pennsylvania, Virginia, and the Carolinas were surpassing Rhode Island as Baptist centers.

In Pennsylvania, the Church of England was concentrated in the eastern counties. Its influence grew steadily in the eighteenth century as wealthy Quakers, including the heirs of William Penn and the proprietors of the colony, converted to it. Anglicans provided the major influence in the founding of the College of Philadelphia (now the University of Pennsylvania)—though the institution, like the colony, was unaffiliated with any denomination.

The adjacent colony of Delaware went through Swedish, Dutch, and finally English control before its residents reluctantly accepted temporary annexation by William Penn's "radical" colony. Delaware's religious profile resembled that of Pennsylvania, but with a greater percentage of Anglicans, fewer Quakers, and only one Swedish Lutheran church (in Wilmington). Like Philadelphia, New Castle and Lewes became major ports of entry for Scots and Scots-Irish Presbyterians.

RELIGION IN THE SOUTHERN COLONIES

In the border colony of Maryland, the foreign travelers would have encountered a colony with an unusual history. Founded in the 1630s by George Calvert, first Lord Baltimore, as a proprietory colony (a grant of land bestowed by the monarch on an individual or group, who then operated it as a commercial venture), Maryland was largely colonized under the direction of two of his sons. Since the Calverts were Roman Catholic, a principal purpose of the colony was to provide a place where other English Roman Catholics could worship freely. An important secondary purpose was to make money for the family—a necessity that required the Calverts to create conditions that would assure steady immigration to their colony. Ironically, by 1770 Maryland had passed through periods of Roman Catholic and Puritan control and had become a colony not only with an Anglican established church but also with laws that imposed severe restrictions against Roman Catholics.

Yet in 1770 the visitors would have found Maryland largely populated by persons who were neither Roman Catholic nor Anglican. The colony contained Irish and Scottish Presbyterians, Quakers, some Baptists, and members of a miscellany of other Protestant churches. So many German Lutherans and Reformed had spilled over from Pennsylvania or landed in Baltimore and relocated that western Maryland resembled the German areas of Pennsylvania. Despite being a minority, Anglicans were highly influential in the colony. By 1770 Maryland's eastern counties were full of Anglican

*Charles Calvert, third Lord Baltimore and
second proprietor of Maryland*

churches whose rectors received such high salaries that clerical applicants for vacancies needed to place their names on a waiting list.

In 1770 the foreign travelers would have found that the Roman Catholics composed approximately ten percent of the colony's population. They would also have noted that Roman Catholics worshiped in churches designed to look like houses. Served by circuit-riding Jesuit priests who often traveled hundreds of miles a week to celebrate private masses, the houses had living quarters at one end and chapels at the other end. The Jesuits themselves owned large tracts of land in the colony, lived and dressed as bachelor gentry, had slaves and indentured servants working on their plantations, and possessed considerable influence.

As for the Roman Catholic laity, they were denied the right to vote or to hold public office during most of the eighteenth century. They had to send their children abroad in "educational convoys" to be educated at Roman Catholic schools. Meanwhile, they paid taxes to support the colony's established Church of England.

Yet Roman Catholics continued to rank among Maryland's leading landowners throughout the colonial period. Except for religion, many were identical in outlook, lifestyle, and even English surnames to the Anglican gentry across the Potomac who composed the First Families of Virginia. Two of these Maryland Roman Catholic gentlemen planters—Charles Carroll (whose fortune was estimated at over £2,000,000) and Daniel Carroll—signed the Declaration of Independence and the Constitution, respectively.

The foreign visitors probably would have seen the religious history of Maryland in a more accurate perspective than some Americans have in the centuries since. At some point in the twentieth century, many Americans came to believe that Maryland was a Roman Catholic colony in inception and population, that it generously offered religious freedom to non-Catholics, and that the famous "Act Concerning Religion" passed by its legislature in 1649 was the world's pioneering act of religious freedom. Ann Landers columns, letters to the editors, and textbooks of American history used in parochial and public schools have lent support to these assertions.

In point of fact, this interpretation of Maryland's history is largely inaccurate. George Calvert established Maryland not only as a place where his fellow Roman Catholics could worship freely but also as a business venture. As an English citizen he was obligated to include Anglicans in the venture, for he received his charter from an Anglican king (Charles I) and kept it at the pleasure of an Anglican parliament. "One can scarcely speak of tolerating in English territory," two church historians write, "a church whose 'supreme governor' was the English monarch."[9] The colony's charter, in fact, presupposed that the Church of England would be Maryland's established church. Although they held the proprietorship, Roman Catholics were dominant in the colony only for a short period. Anglicans were in the majority even on the two ships that carried the first colonists. In the middle of the seventeenth century, Puritans gained substantial control, and the percentage of Roman Catholics steadily decreased as the colony grew.

As the travelers might have learned, the "Act Concerning Religion" of 1649 was passed by a legislature composed of a Protestant majority. It was an act not of religious freedom but of religious toleration—hence its alternate name, the "Maryland Toleration Act." *Religious freedom* means that citizens are free to worship in any way or not at all—and that the state protects that freedom. *Religious toleration* means that the state allows a group to exist and to worship, but retains the right to withdraw or limit that permission at any time. From 1654 to 1661 and from 1692 to the end of the Revolutionary period, Maryland, in fact, nullified its Toleration Act.

Granting religious rights only to Trinitarian Christians, Maryland's act provided for the execution or forfeiture of all lands of any resident who blasphemed or denied the doctrines of the Trinity and the divinity of Christ. It imposed fines, whipping, or imprisonment for any resident who spoke disparagingly of the Virgin Mary, the apostles, or Evangelists. Yet the act strictly enforced tolerance (as long as the act was in force) by punishing any person who dared to offend a Maryland subject by calling them, in a judgmental manner, a host of offensive religious terms, including "heritick, Scismatick, Idolator, puritan, Independent, Prespiterian, popish priest, Jesuite, Jesuited papist, Lutheran, Calvenist, Anabaptist, Brownist, Antinomian, Barrowist, Roundhead, Separatist, or any other name or term in a repoachfull manner relating to matter of Religion"[10] The punishment was ten shillings or public whipping and imprisonment until such time as the aggrieved party was satisfied with the repentance of the offender. Any person who was "willfully to wrong disturbe trouble or molest any person . . . professing to believe in Jesus Christ . . . ." was also strictly punished.[11] Non-Christians were not protected at all.

Despite its limitations and shortcomings, the act represented a major advance for the time. In addition, it reflected a policy that the Calverts had followed from the colony's beginning. As the colonists boarded ships for the voyage to America, George Calvert's instructions included a caveat not to abuse each other about religion. When the colonists arrived in Maryland, Protestants and Roman Catholics initially shared a chapel in St. Mary's City, the colony's first capital.[12]

Thus the Maryland Toleration Act was a pioneering piece of legislation. It came decades before England's own Toleration Act or William Penn's Holy Experiment. Religious toleration generally arose from the Enlightenment, and Maryland's policy of toleration antedates the Enlightenment. But it was an act of limited religious toleration only, and for most of Maryland's colonial history it was not in force. Genuine religious freedom did not come to the United States until the late 1780s. And when it did come, it emerged from the religion of the Founding Fathers.

When the travelers reached Virginia, they would have entered a colony that contained Quakers and Lutherans and small but growing numbers of Presbyterians, Baptists, and Methodists. Directly across the Potomac from Maryland, Virginia also contained a

Roman Catholic mass station and burial ground in Stafford County. But the Church of England was the colony's established church, and in 1770 it was still the church with which most Virginians identified. Thus the College of William and Mary—the first of two colleges established in Virginia in the colonial period—was Anglican. Not until 1775 did the Scots-Irish Presbyterians who settled the Shenandoah Valley found Hampden-Sydney College. Because Anglicanism is so intimately connected with the lives of four of the Founding Fathers included in this study, its doctrines and church life are discussed in detail in the next chapter.

For right or wrong, North Carolina had the reputation as the most irreligious of the American colonies. In the 1730s William Byrd of Virginia declared that North Carolinians had "the least Superstition of any People living. They do not know Sunday from any other day."[13] Several decades prior to Byrd's comment, one of a series of frustrated Anglican missionaries declared that North Carolina contained four kinds of people:

> First the Quakers. . . . Second . . . a great
> many who have no religion, but would be
> Quakers, if by that they were not obliged
> to lead a more moral life. . . . A third sort . . .
> preach and baptize through the country,
> without any manner of orders from any
> sect or pretended Church. A fourth sort,
> who are really zealous for the interest of the
> Church [of England], are the fewest in
> number, but are the better sort of people.[14]

During their travels in 1770, the foreign travelers might have found North Carolina somewhat less irreligious. German Lutherans, German Reformed, and Scots-Irish Presbyterians from Pennsylvania had come down the Shenandoah Valley and settled in the west. The Moravians had established a flourishing center at Salem. Scots Presbyterians and smaller groups of French, Swiss, and Welsh Protestants had immigrated to the eastern part of the colony. The Quakers, who had religion virtually to themselves in North Carolina in the seventeenth century, were declining in prominence but still a significant feature of the religious landscape.

Starting in the 1750s, North Carolina had also become a center of the fervent Separate Baptist movement. A revivalistic and zealous form of Baptists from New England who preached the need for an emotional conversion to Christ, the Separate Baptists used farmer-preachers, itinerant evangelists, and extensive lay witnessing to gather churches throughout the Carolinas and Virginia. Merging with the older forms of the Baptist tradition present in the colonies, they planted the foundation for much of later southern Baptist life and thought. All of these developments should have increased the number of what the Anglican missionary termed "the better sort of people" in North Carolina. Yet Anglicanism itself, though it became the colony's established church in the early eighteenth century, remained a small church whose parishes existed largely on paper.

In South Carolina, the experience of the foreign travelers would have differed. There they would have found an Anglican established church that was in a healthy condition, even though non-Anglicans by 1770 had come to outnumber Anglicans in the colony. Strong and effective lay support and a disarming policy of moderation towards other churches (including Jews) represent two of the reasons the established church remained dominant. Anglicanism was also strengthened by the accession of most of the French Reformed (or Huguenots) who fled to South Carolina and rose to influential positions in its affairs. Other significant religious groups in the colony included the Presbyterians, Lutherans, Quakers, and increasingly the Baptists. All were present from an early date in the cosmopolitan city of Charleston.

Had the visitors left the plantation-centered Low Country and entered the colony's vast backcountry, they would have experienced a situation that more closely resembled that of North Carolina. Settlers poured into this frontier area of South Carolina's piedmont after 1750. But many of its residents were unchurched, the established Anglican church was almost non-existent, and the level of literacy and refinement was low. Even settlements in the backcountry that desired organized religion—such as the several dozen of Presbyterian origin—lacked pastors and had to depend upon the services of occasional missionaries. The one religious group that did well in the backcountry were the Separate Baptists.

In Georgia, the foreign travelers would have visited the most sparsely populated and least prosperous of the thirteen colonies. A product of political necessity and humanitarian idealism, the colony was founded in 1733 as a military buffer zone between Spanish Florida and

South Carolina. It was also intended as a haven for the English poor. In its first decades it attracted not only debtors but also members of religious groups persecuted in Europe, including Jews.

In the middle of the eighteenth century, when this initially experimental colony came under the control of the crown, its Assembly established the Church of England. But like its counterpart in North Carolina, the Anglican establishment in Georgia existed largely on paper. By 1770 Presbyterians, Quakers, Lutherans, other religious groups, and the many irreligious substantially outnumbered Anglicans. In addition, the Separate Baptists were in the wings, ready to flourish in the decades after the Revolution. In an otherwise unremarkable religious history, colonial Georgia stands out for its relationship to three fathers of American evangelicalism—John Wesley, Charles Wesley, and George Whitefield.

D. The Rise of the Evangelical Tradition in America

"Do you know Jesus Christ?," a Moravian bishop asked Oxford don John Wesley while he and his younger brother Charles were serving as Society for the Propagation of the Gospel missionaries to Georgia in the 1730s. An inflexible Anglican whose religion—like that of most Christians of his time—was based upon creeds, sacraments, and good works, Wesley replied that he knew that Christ was the savior of the world. "True," replied the bishop, "but do you know he has saved you?" The Oxford-educated, Greek-reading Wesley had to admit that this was a piece of knowledge he did not pos-

George Whitefield, less impressive in physical appearance than in preaching

sess. "Do you know yourself?," the bishop then added as a final question.

Returning to England after two months and viewing himself (as Charles also regarded himself) as a failure in gaining the sympathy of those to whom he preached, John Wesley underwent a conversion experience in London one evening in 1738. In his words, he felt on that definitive occasion "my heart strangely warmed. I felt I did believe in Christ, in Christ alone for salvation; and an assurance was given me that He had taken away my sins, even mine, and saved me from the law of sin and death."

A few days earlier, his brother Charles had experienced a similar conversion. The two Wesleys now formed the Methodist movement—a highly disciplined, conversion-centered, and largely lay movement in the Church of England. It took its name from the methodically pious "Holy Club" the then high-church Wesleys had founded while at Oxford. John Wesley hoped that "the people called Methodists" would act as an evangelical yeast to lift not only the established church but also all of the British Isles to "vital, practical religion" and to the practice of "Scriptural holiness."

John was the movement's principal organizer and preacher. Charles supported it by writing thousands of hymns. Whitefield, a protégé of the Wesleys at Oxford who had followed them to Georgia, became one of the most dramatic and effective evangelists in the history of Christianity. Making seven trips to colonial America, preaching in fields as well as churches, often preaching thirty days a month and four times a Sunday, he attracted huge crowds that would stand in rapt silence to hear his sermons. A farmer's account of a visit of Whitefield to Connecticut in 1740 illustrates the great excitement that the young evangelical's preaching created:

> One morning… there came a messenger
> and said Mr. Whitfeld… is to preach at
> Middletown this morning at 10 o clock. I
> was in my field at work [and] I dropt my
> tool… and run home …and bade my
> wife to get ready quick to goo and hear
> Mr. Whitfeld I brought my hors home
> and soon mounted and took my wife up
> and went forward as fast as I thought the

hors could bear.... We improved every moment to get along as if we was fleeing for our lives, all this while fearing we should be too late to hear the Sarmon, for we had twelve miles to ride double in littel more than an hour. . . .

I saw before me a Cloud or fog rising—I first thought—off from the great river. But as I came nearer the road I heard a noise, something like a low rumbling thunder, and I presently found it was the rumbling of horses feet coming down the road and this Cloud was a Cloud of dust made by the running of horses feet.... And when I came nearer it was like a stedy streem of horses and their riders.... Every hors semed to go with all his might to carry his rider to hear the news from heaven for the saving of their Souls. It made me trembel to see the Sight. . .I herd no man speak a word all the way . . . but evry one presing forward in great haste.

And when we gat down to the old meating house, thare was a great multitude. It was said to be 3 or 4000 people assembled together.... I turned and looked toward the great river and saw the fery boats running swift … bringing over loads of people.... Everything—men, horses and boats—all

seamed to be struglin for life. The land and
the banks over the river looked black with
people and horse all along the 12 miles. I
see no man at work in his field, but all
seamed to be gone.

Mr. Whitfeld... looked almost angellical—
a young, slim, slender youth before some
thousands of people, and with a bold,
undaunted countenance. And my hearing
how God was with him everywhere. . .it
solomnized my mind, and put me in a
trembling fear before he began to preach,
for he looked as if he was Cloathed with
authority from the great God.... and my
hearing him preach gave me a heart wound,
by god's blessing. My old foundation was
broken up and I saw that my righteousness
would not save me. Then I was convinced
of the doctrine of Election...because all that
I could do would not save me, and he
[God] had decreed from Eternity who
should be saved and who not....[15]

An Anglican Calvinist, Whitefield preached an eloquent but simple message—that his listeners must
confront the terrifying realization that they deserve
damnation and can be saved from Hell only through the
grace and forgiveness of God. In gratitude for God's forgiveness, they must be born again, become new men or
women in Christ Jesus, and live a reformed life. This was

the message of what came to be called "Evangelicalism," an interpretation of Christianity that would sweep across America in later centuries and influence many denominations.

Benjamin Franklin (who not only knew Whitefield but also printed his sermons and journals) held markedly different religious views from those of Whitefield. Yet even Franklin fell under the "Grand Itinerant's" spell when Whitefield appealed in Philadelphia for funds for an orphanage he wished to establish in Georgia but build with materials and workmen from Pennsylvania:

> I thought it would have been better to
> have built the house here, and brought the
> children to it. This I advis'd; but he . . .
> rejected my counsel, and I therefore refus'd
> to contribute. I happened soon after to
> attend one of his sermons, in the course of
> which I perceived he intended to finish
> with a collection, and I silently resolved he
> should get nothing from me. I had in my
> pocket a handful of copper money, three
> or four silver dollars, and five pistoles in
> gold. As he proceded I began to soften,
> and concluded to give the coppers.
> Another stroke of his oratory made me
> asham'd of that, and determin'd me to give
> the silver; and he finish'd so admirably,
> that I empty'd my pocket wholly into the
> collector's dish, gold and all.[16]

Franklin not only admired Whitefield's oratorical ability but also liked him personally. Franklin accommodated him at his home, profited monetarily from publishing Whitefield's writing, and corresponded with him for more than three decades after their first meeting in Philadelphia. One biographer has counted forty-five descriptions of Whitefield's preaching in the weekly issues of Franklin's Gazette as well as eight front pages that included the texts of Whitefield's sermons.[17]

The ordination of Francis Asbury in 1784 as "general superintendent" marked the beginning of Methodism as a separate American denomination.

Whitefield died in 1770, the year in which the foreign visitors came to the colonies.

Along with Congregationalist minister Jonathan Edwards, Whitefield personified the Great Awakening, the wave of religious revivals that swept the American colonies beginning in the 1730s and 1740s and emphasized "the new birth" or personal experience of the grace of God. "Hard to define, being one of those popular movements which have no obvious beginning or end, no pitched battles or legal victories with specific dates, no constitutions or formal leaders, no easily quantifiable statistics and no formal set of beliefs," the Great Awakening was nevertheless the single most transforming event in the religious history of colonial America.[18] It left the legacy of evangelical "born-again" Christianity. Although the awakening affected many churches, the Baptists and Methodists were its greatest heirs.

At the time of the visit of the foreign travelers, Methodism had gained substantial converts and some influence in the British Isles. In the American colonies, however, it was still a small movement. Emotional, conversion-centered, largely lower-class in constituency, it taught a message of free will and of the possibility of salvation for all humans (and not just for the elect). It was served by lay preachers sent from England by Wesley, the first of whom had arrived in the colonies only in 1769. Thus until it separated in 1784 from Anglicanism, Methodism existed in America as a small ultra-evangelical wing of the Church of England. Yet along with the Baptists, it represented the future of American Protestantism. Below the Mason-Dixon line, the Baptist and Methodist interpretations of Christianity became the folk religion of the American South. And in the rural areas and small towns of nineteenth-century America, the Methodist circuit rider became a familiar figure.

In 1770 Baptist and Methodist Christianity also represented the religious future of African-Americans. To a far greater extent than in the Caribbean or in Roman Catholic Latin America, the forms of religion the slaves brought from Africa were suppressed in the Protestant atmosphere of the American colonies. From the seventeenth century on, various colonial Protestant churches baptized and catechized a small percentage of the colonies' blacks. In contrast to the visible presence of a small minority of blacks in white churches, African-Americans mixed some ancestral practices and beliefs with Christianity in their "Invisible Institution" of secret, unrecorded worship.

The Great Awakening of the 1730s and 1740s, however, caused the widespread evangelization not only of poor whites and Indians but also of enslaved and free blacks. The Awakening's message of the "new birth" resonated with the American experience of blacks as well as with some aspects of their African religious background. Yet the emergence of separate congregations of black Baptists is generally dated to the early 1770s, and the founding of the first black denomination—the African Methodist Episcopal Church—did not occur until the late 1780s. The emergence of the form of religious music called "Spirituals"—in which African-Americans adapted evangelical Protestantism to meet their own needs and to keep alive their hopes for freedom—also occurred largely in the nineteenth century.

Thus the foreign travelers of 1770, as well as the six Founding Fathers covered in this study, would have had little contact with African-American Christianity. In addition, they would have known relatively little about the Baptists, Methodists, or Roman Catholics— the three religious groups that became so prominent in the United States in the nineteenth century. The Founders knew Roman Catholicism in America only through fleeting associations, though most were well aware of its European history. Those like Franklin, Adams, Jefferson, and Monroe who served the new nation in France experienced Roman Catholicism first hand.

Only the southerners would have had any experience with black religion, and it would have been limited. None of the Founding Fathers were evangelicals, although Madison attended a moderately evangelical Episcopal church in the last years of his life. In fact, James Monroe was offended by an evangelical sermon during his presidential tour of 1817, and John Adams belonged to the anti-Great Awakening wing of Congregationalism—much of which later became Unitarian.[19]

Finally, none of the Founding Fathers knew anything of the churches that became so large in the United States in the twentieth century— the Pentecostals (or charismatics) and the non-denominational evangelicals. What the six Founding Fathers did know were the churches in which they had been raised—and in all cases those churches were the established churches of their colonies. But the Founders were also very familiar with a radical religious outlook called Deism, to which this study now turns. ❖

2. THE ANGLICAN TRADITION AND
THE VIRGINIA FOUNDING FATHERS

o discuss the religion of the Founding Fathers means to discuss religion in the United States of their time. Washington, Jefferson, Madison, and Monroe were born and baptized in what Virginians of the time called "the Church," "the Church of England," "the Established Church," or "the Church of Virginia." The independence of the thirteen colonies from the United Kingdom prompted the American members of the Church of England to discard the word "England." In its place they adopted the term "Episcopal" (essentially meaning "we have bishops") and named their denomination "The Protestant Episcopal Church in the United States of America."

The name "Episcopal" traced back to the tumultuous Commonwealth period in English history, when clergy and laity who desired continued rule by bishops used that term for themselves. To some extent, members of the Church of England used it for their church during the colonial period. In later centuries the term *Anglican* (from the Latin for "English") came into common use to describe churches in any country that held the faith and practice of the Church of England. This book will use the terms *Church of England*, *Established Church*, and *Anglican* interchangeably, but will generally employ the word *Episcopal* when discussing that church following the revolution.

Throughout the colonial period, the Church of England was the established church of colonial Virginia.

President James Madison of William and Mary, teacher of Monroe and close friend of Jefferson, Franklin, and other Founding Fathers

Colonial Virginians were born into the Anglican faith just as they were born into the English nation. The Virginia General Assembly legislated for the established church, supported it through taxation, and protected it against competition.

State churches represented the norm in European Christianity beginning in the fourth century. Of the thirteen colonies, nine—or almost seventy per cent—had established churches. Congregationalism (or the faith of the Puritans) was established in New Hampshire, Massachusetts, and Connecticut. Anglicanism was established in the lower counties of New York, as well as in Maryland, Virginia, North Carolina, South Carolina, and Georgia. It was strong, however, only in Maryland, Virginia, and South Carolina.

A form of Christianity that claims to blend the best of Christian teachings and practice from the periods of the apostles, the church fathers, and the Reformation, Anglicanism emerged from the English Reformation of the sixteenth and seventeenth centuries. Like Roman Catholicism and Eastern Orthodoxy, it kept a hierarchical ministry of bishops, priests, and deacons and maintained a formal style of worship. Like those churches, its members used a mass book, or book of prayers and rites. Titled the "Book of Common Prayer," it was intended to reproduce the worship and teachings of early Christianity.

But like Protestant churches, the Church of England held that Holy Scripture—not the teachings of popes or church councils—was the final authority for Christian belief. It accepted the authority of the early

General Councils and emphasized the Apostles, Nicene, and Athanasian creeds as standards of faith precisely because it believed their teachings were true to Scripture. Like the continental Protestant churches and unlike Roman Catholicism and Eastern Orthodoxy, it believed that churches could err in their teachings. "There was never any thing by the wit of man so well devised, or so sure established, which in continuance of time hath not been corrupted," the preface to the first Book of Common Prayer asserted in 1549.

Anglicanism can best be viewed as what Queen Elizabeth I and her theologians desired it to be. They attempted to make the Church of England a middle way—or *via media*—between Roman Catholicism and Calvinism, the two interpretations of Christianity that contended for control of England in the Reformation period. Anglican theologians asserted that Roman Catholicism had added too much man-made doctrine to Christianity. They believed that the teachings of the Swiss Reformer John Calvin, or Calvinism—which had won over Scotland and was embodied in England by the Puritans—had subtracted too much that was important to Christianity. With England divided between these two views, and with many citizens desiring only an end to conflict, Elizabeth and her advisors tried to steer a middle course patterned upon early Christianity.

Finding the middle course is one thing and keeping to it is another. Thus it was not surprising that the Church of England quickly developed parties, or factions. The *high-church* party wanted the national church to tack more towards Eastern Orthodoxy and Roman

Catholicism. The *low-church* party wanted to move Anglican faith and practice closer to Calvinism and Lutheranism. Largely, however, the Church of England remained what it had become during the reign of Elizabeth—a church more Catholic than the continental Protestant churches, but one substantially more Protestant than the Catholic churches centered around Rome and Constantinople. It claimed to be a unique synthesis of Catholicism and Protestantism.

Anglicanism came to Virginia in 1607, first at Jamestown and then in ever-widening settlements along Virginia's rivers and newly-created roads. Whenever settlers moved too far from existing courthouses and parishes, the General Assembly of Virginia simply established new counties and new parishes. *Parishes* were geographical districts, perhaps 150 square miles in size, containing two to four Anglican churches, a minister called a *rector*, and a governing body of self-perpetuating laymen called a *vestry* headed by two *churchwardens*. Gradually parishes containing substantial churches of Gothic or Georgian design dotted Virginia. By the start of the American Revolution, Virginia's Established Church had some 250 churches spread over 100 parishes stretching as far west as Kentucky.

This church provided the religious background out of which Washington, Jefferson, Madison, and Monroe—as well as such Founding Fathers as Patrick Henry, George Mason, and George Wythe—emerged. The earliest religious memories of these men would have revolved around the wood or brick church their family attended on Sundays. Most of their fathers

James Monroe was married in and later buried from his wife's home church, Trinity Church, New York City

would have served as vestrymen of their parishes. In due time, the Founding Fathers would have assumed the same position. The parish priest—or parson—would have been a familiar figure to them, and they would have received much of their early education at academies run by Anglican clergy.

Additionally, the words and cadences of the Book of Common Prayer—"Almighty and most merciful Father: we have erred and strayed from thy ways like lost sheep.... We thine unworthy servants do give thee most humble and hearty thanks for all thy goodness and loving-kindness to us.... Ye that do truly and earnestly repent you of your sins, and are in love and charity with your neighbors...draw near with faith, and take this holy Sacrament to your comfort.... Fulfil now, O Lord, the desires and petitions of thy servants, as many be most expedient for them; granting us in this world knowledge of thy truth, and in the world to come life everlasting. Amen."—ran in their blood.

The Anglican faith of Virginia differed from the New England Puritanism out of which Adams and Franklin emerged. Both Adams and Franklin changed their religious views and embraced a form of Deism. So, too, did Washington, Jefferson, Madison, and Monroe. But all of these men, except Franklin, continued to worship at least occasionally in the church of their ancestors. They married under its auspices, consigned their children to its care, and were buried by its clergy. The impress of their religious background remained strong, even though their questioning of certain of their church's fundamental doctrines led them to Deism. ✤

3. THE ENLIGHTENMENT RELIGION OF DEISM

"*T*he religion of Deism is superior to the Christian Religion," the radical Deist Thomas Paine declared:

It is free from all those invented and torturing articles that shock our reason ... with which the Christian religion abounds. Its creed is pure and sublimely simple. It believes in God, and there it rests. It honours Reason as the choicest gift of God to man and the faculty by which he is enabled to contemplate the power, wisdom, and goodness of the Creator displayed in the creation; And reposing itself on his protection, both here and hereafter, it avoids all presumptuous beliefs and rejects, as the fabulous inventions of men, all books pretending to revelation. [20]

"The Deists," an American clergyman wrote:

... were never organized into a sect, had no creed or form of worship, recognized no leader, and were constantly shifting their ground. ... so that it is impossible to include them strictly under any definition.

The cleric went on to attempt "as near a definition as possible":

Deism is what is left of Christianity after
casting off everything that is peculiar to it.
The Deist is one who denies the Divinity, the
Incarnation, and the Atonement of Christ, and
the work of the Holy Ghost; who denies the
God of Israel, and believes in the God of nature.[21]

From the late seventeenth century on, a school of
religious thought called *Deism* existed in England and
on the continent. It emerged from the Enlightenment, a
complex movement of ideas marked by an emphasis on
reason as well as a self-confident challenge of traditional
political, religious, and social ideas. The scientific and
philosophical work of three Englishmen—Francis
Bacon, Isaac Newton, and John Locke—undergirded
the English Enlightenment.

A philosopher and lawyer, Bacon insisted that
observation and experience—not abstract principles—
provided the only true foundations of human knowledge. Applying Bacon's methodology to science, Isaac
Newton, the leading physicist of his time, concentrated
on discovering and reporting immutable laws of nature.
For Bacon a "first cause" created the universe, which
operated according to natural laws. Locke, a philosopher, argued that human experience and rationality—
rather than religious dogma and mystery—determined
the validity of human beliefs. Locke's test of truth was
whether a belief made sense to human reason.

Bacon, Newton, and Locke were all Anglicans of
varying degrees of orthodoxy. But their work and those
of other philosophers and scientists provided the

foundation for Deism's new understanding of the universe and of human life. "There arose in our society," the historian Crane Brinton wrote, "what seems to me clearly to be a new religion, certainly related to, descended from, and by many reconciled with, Christianity. I call this religion simply Enlightenment, with a capital *E*." [22]

During the eighteenth century and into the nineteenth, Deism had adherents throughout continental Europe, the British Isles, and the American colonies. It became the creed of Holy Roman Emperor Joseph II and of Frederick the Great of Prussia. Because it was guided by individual reason, the movement was neither organized nor uniform. Thus some Deists renounced Christian belief more thoroughly than others.

Personified in England, France, and America by such controversial figures as Anthony Collins, Voltaire (Francois-Marie Arouët), and Thomas Paine, the movement's radical wing viewed Christianity as a barrier to moral improvement and to social justice. In successive books and tracts written early in the eighteenth century, Collins defended the use of reason. He found fraud in one part of the Church of England's statement of faith, attacked clergy of all denominations, argued that the Bible commanded free inquiry, and denied any relationship between Old Testament prophecies and the life of Jesus of Nazareth. The keen-witted Voltaire satirized competing philosophical systems, argued for the use of reason as common sense, and spread Locke's ideas on political and religious tolerance. Perhaps no writer has attacked dogmatic Christianity more effectively.

The son of an English Quaker artisan, Paine immigrated to the American colonies in his late thirties. He became well known for his pamphlets supporting the movement for independence from England. When he temporarily moved to France in the 1790s to assist the French Revolution, Paine lived in home of James Monroe in Paris, while Monroe served as Minister to France. Like other Founding Fathers, Monroe had been impressed by Paine's patriotic writings during the Revolutionary War; the pamphleteer had befriended not only Monroe but also Franklin, Jefferson, Adams, and Washington (though Paine later broke with the last two).

Arrested on contrived charges during the French Reign of Terror, Paine was one of many persons released from Paris prisons through Monroe's adroit interventions. Long months in prison had left him in bad health, and the Monroes took him into their residence in Paris to convalesce. For two years (substantially longer than Monroe had anticipated), Paine recuperated with the Monroe family and participated in their social circle. He and Monroe formed a close friendship that lasted until Paine's death in 1809. The two men may have discussed religion frequently, and it is not idle to speculate that Monroe's views moved further away from Christian orthodoxy during this period.

Written during 1793 and 1794, partially in a French jail and partially at Monroe's home, Paine's *The Age of Reason* (published in 1794-95) helped to popularize Deism in the United States. Paine wrote the second part (which deals with the Bible) using a King James Version borrowed from the Monroes. Because it mercilessly assaulted and lampooned Judeo-Christian beliefs—for Paine organized Christianity had been a negative influence on world history—the book alienated many of his previous supporters. To orthodox American Christians, Paine became a villain and an "infidel."

The Age of Reason denied "that the Almighty ever did communicate anything to man, by any mode of speech, in any language, or by any kind of vision." Paine termed Christianity "a fable, which, for absurdity and extravagance is not exceeded by any thing that is to be found in the mythology of the ancients." The book's hammer-like approach to the Bible is displayed by its treatment of a passage in the Gospel of Matthew that depicts deceased followers of Jesus rising from their graves and going into Jerusalem after the crucifixion:

> The writer…should have told us who the
> saints were…and what became of them
> afterward…whether they came out naked
> …or…full dressed, and where they got
> their dresses; whether they went to their former
> habitations, and reclaimed their wives, their
> husbands, and their property, and how they
> were received; whether they…brought
> actions of *crim. con.* against the rival
> interlopers; …whether they died again, or
> went back to their graves alive, and buried
> themselves.… [23]

Other Deists tried to reconcile Deism with Christianity. Viewing themselves as Christians, they went to church, prayed, and assigned a salvatory role to

Jesus. Certain clergy in the Christian churches of France, the British Isles, Germany, America, and other countries held Deistic views in the eighteenth century. Deists were found even in Roman Catholic pews and pulpits in Maryland.

Regardless of where they fell on the Deist spectrum, many Deists continued to respect the moral teachings of Jesus without believing in his divine status. But the tendency of Deism was to emphasize ethical endeavors— hence the concern of most Deists for social justice and their profound opposition to all forms of tyranny. In addition, they replaced the Judeo-Christian explanation of existence with a religion far more oriented to reason and nature than to the Hebrew Bible, Christian Testament, and Christian creeds. In the understanding of the typical Deist, a rational "Supreme Architect"—one of a variety of terms Deists used for the deity—created the earth and human life. This omnipotent and unchangeable creator then withdrew to let events take their course on earth without further interference.

Just as a ticking watch presupposes a watchmaker, so Deists thought that the rational, mechanistic harmony of nature revealed a deity. The Deistic view of nature was so high that men such as Ethan Allen and Paine could write of it as God's revelation. "Are we to have no word of God—no revelation?," Paine asked in the *Age of Reason*. Paine responded to his own question: "I answer, yes; there is a word of God; there is a revelation. *The word of God is the creation we behold, and it is in this word,* which no human invention can counterfeit or alter, that God speaketh universally to man." [24]

Whereas the principal revelation for Christianity—the Bible—bore every sign of human counterfeiting or alteration, Deists saw the magnificent design of nature as revealing a Creator, or what Thomas Jefferson termed "a superattending power." Some Deists even employed rhapsodic terms to describe nature—"All loving and All-lovely, All-divine" or "righteous and immortal."[25] Writing in 1815, an aging American poet of Deistic belief praised nature in similar words:

All that we see, about, abroad,
What is it all, but nature's God?
In meaner works discovered here
No less than in the starry sphere. . . .

In all the attributes divine
Unlimited perfectings shine;
In these enwrapt, in these complete,
All virtues in that centre meet.[26]

To be sure, when citizens of the twenty-first century look at nature, they may see not simply majesty, order, and beauty but also earthquakes, tornadoes, hurricanes, and famine. But at a time when most people thought that the world was thousands rather than millions of years old, Deists could more easily see nature as bearing the impress of a Maker. Governed by reason—which Paine called "the most formidable weapon against errors of every kind"—the human mind possessed the ability to comprehend the natural laws God had initiated.

COMMON SENSE;

ADDRESSED TO THE

INHABITANTS

OF

AMERICA,

On the following interesting

SUBJECTS.

I. Of the Origin and Design of Government in general,
with concise Remarks on the English Constitution.

II. Of Monarchy and Hereditary Succession.

III. Thoughts on the present State of American Affairs.

IV. Of the present Ability of America, with some
miscellaneous Reflections.

WRITTEN BY AN ENGLISHMAN.

THE SECOND EDITION.

Man knows no Master save creating HEAVEN,
Or those whom choice and common good ordain.

THOMSON.

PHILADELPHIA;
Printed, and Sold, by R. BELL, in Third-Street.

MDCCLXXVI.

John Adams's copy of Thomas Paine's Common Sense

Though technically not a Deist, Edward Herbert, first Lord Herbert of Cherbury, formulated the classic five points of Deism in the seventeenth century. Herbert stated that (1) there is a God; (2) he ought to be worshiped; (3) virtue is the principal element in this worship; (4) humans should repent for their sins; and (5) there is a life after death, where the evil will be punished, and the good rewarded. Herbert's reduction of the essence of religion to these five points as well as his rejection of revelation causes many historians to view him as the forerunner, or father, of the movement.

This five-point program is far from atheism. For that reason, Theodore Roosevelt's later description of Paine as "a filthy little atheist" was incorrect. Paine actually wrote *The Age of Reason* as an antidote for the atheism that was sweeping revolutionary France. In his mind, Christianity was the infidel, and he was the faithful believer. Declaring *The Age of Reason* his "profession of faith," Paine wrote:

> I believe in one God, and no more; and I hope
> for happiness beyond this life. I believe in the
> equality of man and I believe that religious duties
> consist in doing justice, loving mercy, and
> endeavoring to make our fellow-creatures happy.[27]

Yet if a reader cannot call Deism "atheistic," it is equally impossible to call the movement "Christian." Deists repeatedly called into question any teaching or belief of Christianity that they could not reconcile with human reason. Reason for them was paramount for determining religious truth. Thus Elihu Palmer, a former Presbyterian minister who became a leading American Deist, not only published a treatise entitled *Reason, the Glory of Our Nature*, but also edited a newspaper called the *Temple of Reason*. In 1784, Ethan Allen, the Revolutionary War hero from Vermont, published *Reason: the Only Oracle of Man*. On this basis many Deists dismissed the doctrines of the Trinity (the teaching that God exists in the three persons of Father, Son, and Holy Spirit), the incarnation (the assertion that God took human nature and form in the person of Jesus of Nazareth), the virgin birth (the belief that the Holy Spirit was the father of Jesus and the Virgin Mary his mother), and the resurrection (the declaration that Jesus physically rose from the grave after his crucifixion and burial).

Additionally, they found belief in biblical revelation —the concept that the Bible revealed God and God's will—faulty when subjected to rational analysis. Paine and other left-wing Deists found the Bible a pastiche of magic, superstition, irrationality, pre-scientific thinking, and bloodthirsty ethics. Because they believed that only an imperfect God would suspend his universal laws to perform "irrational" acts, they dismissed the miracles recorded in the Bible. Paine found the doctrine of the atonement—the Christian teaching that Christ died on behalf of sinful humanity—so irrational that he declared he could not fathom how anyone in possession of full faculties could honestly believe in it.

Moreover, most Deists differed from the Judeo-Christian tradition in their concept of God. Judaism and Christianity asserted that a God named YHWH had revealed himself to Moses at Mt. Sinai. This God was the God of Abraham, Isaac, Jacob, Joseph, David, Solomon, the Prophets, John the Baptist, and Jesus of Nazareth. He was a God whom the Bible depicts as acting in history and hearing prayers.

In place of this Hebrew God, Deists postulated a distant deity to whom they referred with terms such as "the First Cause," "the Creator of the Universe," "the Divine Artist," "the Divine Author of All Good," "the Grand Architect," "the God of Nature," "Nature's God," "Divine Providence," and (in a phrase used by Franklin) "the Author and Owner of our System." The Declaration of Independence displays precisely this kind of wording.

Thus Deism inevitably undermined the personal religion of the Judeo-Christian tradition. In the world view of the typical Deist, humans had no need to read the Bible, to pray, to be baptized or circumcized, to receive Holy Communion, to attend church or synagogue, or to heed the words or ministrations of misguided priests, ministers, or rabbis. They needed no personal relationship with Jesus Christ. In his tract, *The Religion of Nature Delineated*, the English Deist William Wollaston declared that humans would learn more truths about religion if they studied nature and science rather than the Bible and Christian theology.

But many Deists went further than simply absenting themselves from religious rites. They criticized not only the Judeo-Christian tradition but also all organized religion for fostering divisive sectarianism, for encouraging persecution, and for stifling freedom of thought and speech throughout history. "Persecution is not an original feature in any religion," Paine wrote "but it is always the strongly marked feature of all...religions established by law." [28] As the French philosopher Denis Diderot's hyperbolic words—"let us strangle the last king with the guts of the last priest"—indicate, Deists despised political and religious despotism. [29] Their fundamental belief in reason and equality drove them to embrace liberal political ideals. In the eighteenth century, many Deists advocated universal education, freedom of the press, and separation of church and state. These principles are commonplace in the twenty-first century, but were radical in the eighteenth.

Today some aspects of Deism are continued in the United States in the Masonic order, in the Unitarian-Universalist denomination, in the Ethical Culture movement, in the historical-critical approach to the Bible that emerged in the late nineteenth century, in the tradition of free thought, and to some extent in the Religious Society of Friends (or Quakers). The spirit of rational inquiry, of skepticism about dogma, and of religious toleration that animated Deism continues to influence the religious views of many persons who occupy pews in churches and synagogues. ✢

4. THE FOUNDING FATHERS AND DEISM

*D*eism proved influential in the United States from roughly 1725 through the first decades of the nineteenth century. Among educated eighteenth-century Americans, the idea of reason as a liberator from the shackles of repressive government and religion won widespread acclaim. By the 1750s, orthodox clergy had begun to warn against the movement. Deism became especially fashionable at American colleges in the decades immediately following the Revolution. In those decades Enlightenment rationalism unseated Christian orthodoxy at Yale, Harvard, and other denominational colleges.

In Virginia, the center of Deism was William and Mary, the alma mater of Monroe and Jefferson, and the institution where Washington also served as chancellor. "At the end of the century, the College of William and Mary was regarded as the hotbed of infidelity and of the wild politics of France," an orthodox Episcopalian remembered:

> The intimacy produced between infidel
> France and our own country, by the union
> of our arms against the common foe, was
> most baneful in its influence with our citizens
> generally, and on none more than those of
> Virginia. The grain of mustard-seed which
> was planted at Williamsburg, about the
> middle of the century, had taken root there
> and sprung up and spread its branches over
> the whole State.[30]

Students and young people generally embrace novelty and new ideas. Thus it would be surprising if Deism had not influenced the Founding Fathers; most were young men when the movement began to spread. Washington and Adams were born in the 1730s, Jefferson in the 1740s, and Madison and Monroe in the 1750s.

The Founding Fathers began their college studies during the formative years of Deism. Adams attended Harvard in the 1750s; Jefferson studied at William and Mary in the 1760s, while Monroe enrolled there in the 1770s; and though Washington never attended college, he moved in the circles of gentry who had been educated at William and Mary and at other colleges.

Only Madison attended a college (the College of New Jersey, later renamed Princeton) known for most of the eighteenth century for its Christian orthodoxy. Yet after Madison returned to Virginia, his religious beliefs clearly moved in a Deistic direction. An orthodox opponent of Deism who knew the disposition of the Madison family attributed the young squire's change to "political associations with those of infidel principles, of whom there were many in his day." [31]

As these words indicate, Deism influenced, in one way or another, most of the political leaders who designed the new American government. Since the Founding Fathers did not hold identical views on religion, they should not be lumped together. But if census takers trained in Christian theology had set up broad categories in 1790 labeled "Atheism," "Deism and Unitarianism," "Orthodox Protestantism," "Orthodox Roman

Catholicism," and "Other," and if they had interviewed Franklin, Washington, Adams, Jefferson, Madison, and Monroe, they would undoubtedly have placed every one of these six Founding Fathers in some way under the category of "Deism and Unitarianism." ❖

5. THE RELIGIOUS VIEWS OF
BENJAMIN FRANKLIN

*J*ndustrious, temperate but outspoken, possessor of
an almost pixyish humor, Benjamin Franklin was
the first prominent American Deist and the most
universal American of his time. Although Franklin grew
up in the ethos of Calvinist New England, his youth
coincided with the introduction of British Deistic
thought into the colonies.

Franklin's father, a candlemaker, sent his son at age
eight to Boston Latin School (where many Puritan
divines studied), probably because he intended the young
man for the Congregationalist ministry. But no stories
from Benjamin's youth depict him as pious or faithful;
rather, others described him as "skeptical, puckish. . . and
irreverent."[32] Removed after a year by his father from the
Latin School and enrolled in a writing and arithmetic
academy, Benjamin ultimately educated himself from the
age of ten on. Thus he never attended college, though he
later received numerous honorary degrees (including the
first one awarded by William and Mary). Franklin tried
on various theological positions while young, but came
to view theology as a discipline that often focused on
petty distinctions rather than on broader truths.

Although young Franklin's voracious reading
included defenses of the Calvinist tradition in which
he had been raised, he found Deistic authors more
persuasive. "Franklin adopted much from deism that
would have alienated him from Puritanism," one of his
biographers asserted, "but nothing from Puritanism that

Benjamin Franklin, prudent Deist

would be incompatible with deism."[33] By the age of fifteen, he had become a convinced Deist. By seventeen, he had already read such representative Deistic writers as Locke, Collins, Joseph Addison, and Locke's patron, the third Earl of Shaftesbury. By nineteen, during a two-year stay in London, he had published a pamphlet on morality that brought him to the attention of English Deists, though he later repudiated its radicalism.

Franklin's new Deistic views and his absence from church services unsettled not only his parents but also such religious figures as Boston's Puritan patriarch Increase Mather. Some of the aphorisms in *Poor Richard's Almanack*, which Franklin published from 1732 to 1757, display his Deistic concern that good beliefs beget good works. "Sin is not hurtful because it is forbidden," he wrote in the Almanac in 1739, "but it is forbidden because it is hurtful. . . . Nor is a Duty beneficial because it is commanded, but it is commanded, because it is beneficial." In other passages Poor Richard observes in good Deistic fashion: "Many have quarreled about religion that never practiced it." At another point he declares that "serving God is doing good to man, but praying is thought an easier service and therefore is more generally chosen."

Despite his break with orthodoxy, Franklin retained some of the Calvinist views he had been taught. Although his Deistic religion was free from the agonized concern and introspection about salvation that characterized Calvinism, Franklin's diligence, frugality, and dislike of religious pretension can fairly be seen as carryovers from his background. "No man 'er was glorious, who was not laborious," he had Poor Richard opine in 1734 in words that recall the Puritan teaching about calling and work ethic.

Similarly, Calvinists insisted that sin infuses all human thoughts and actions. Thus it is not surprising that Franklin remained skeptical about the claims advanced by Enlightenment writers about the innate goodness and ultimate perfectability of humanity.

Calvinism was sufficiently influential that he chose as his first church home in Philadelphia (where he moved in 1723) the Presbyterian Church, the closest body in doctrine and practice to his inherited Congregationalism. With its apparent affirmation of the resurrection of the body, the epitaph he wrote for himself as a young printer also seems to display his background in orthodox Christianity:

The body of
B. Franklin, Printer;
(like the cover of an old book,
Its contents worn out,
and stripped of its lettering and gilding)
Lies here, food for worms.
But the work shall not be lost:
For it will, (as he believed) appear once more,
In a new and more elegant edition,
Revised and corrected
By the Author.

Franklin was also among those Deists who remained open to the possibility of divine intervention or special providence in human affairs. As he wrote in an essay in the 1730s, God "sometimes interferes by His particular providence and sets aside the effects which would otherwise have been produced by . . . causes."[34]

Unlike radical, or anti-Christian Deists, Franklin perceived that organized religion could benefit society by encouraging public virtue as well as by promoting social order. He believed in a benevolent Creator, whom humans should worship through virtuous behavior. Thus Franklin urged his daughter Sarah to "go constantly to church." He himself was an infrequent churchgoer. But since he developed a certain fondness for ceremony and ritual, the church he most frequently attended was Christ Church, one of Philadelphia's three Episcopal churches. He did so despite being at odds with the ruling Penn family, many of whom had become Episcopalian. One of the several reasons Franklin seems to have befriended George Whitefield may have stemmed from the discomfiting effect Whitefield's evangelical preaching had on the stodgy elites of Philadelphia.

Franklin's American protégé Paine (whom he had met in England and persuaded to emigrate to the colonies) became a propagandist for Deism. But Franklin did not. He would satirize, but seldom directly criticize, other religious faiths. Although Franklin privately questioned such Christian doctrinal teachings as the incarnation, the Trinity, and the resurrection, he remained cautious when discussing them publicly. Thus his religious views display not dogmatism but rather tentativeness and ambivalence. Prudent and tolerant, he contributed to the construction budgets not only of every church in Philadelphia but also of the city's one synagogue.

This ambivalence towards dogma fostered Franklin's conviction that no system of thought is wholly right or entirely wrong. As a result, Franklin (like other Deists) came to believe that religious toleration was vital to a free society. When his grandson was unable to marry a young woman in France because her parents opposed her marrying a Protestant, Franklin's view was that religious differences did not matter in marriage, in that all religions were basically the same.

Insatiably curious, ambivalent about religion, prudent in his declarations about it, offended by dogmatism and intolerance, opposed to the highly emotional conversion experiences of the Great Awakening, Franklin made morality primary in his interpretation of religion. Like other Deists, he believed that humans served God best when they performed good works on behalf of humanity and society. "I think vital religion has always suffered," Franklin wrote to his parents shortly after his thirtieth birthday, "when orthodoxy is more regarded than virtues." He once defined "a good Christian" as someone who is "a good Parent, a good Child, a good Husband or Wife, a good Neighbour or Friend, a good Subject or citizen."[35] He wrote a liturgy that emphasized morality, and he worked hard to infuse morality into the common life of Philadelphia.

Five weeks before his death, when he received an inquiry about his religious beliefs from a Congregationalist minister who was president of Yale College, Franklin replied:

> Here is my Creed. I believe in one God,
> Creator of the Universe: That he governs
> the World by his Providence. That he
> ought to be worshiped. That the most
> acceptable Service we can render to him,
> is doing good to his other Children. That
> the Soul of Man is immortal, and will be

treated with Justice in another life,
respecting its Conduct in this. These I
take to be the fundamental Principles of
all sound Religion.

Morality remained primary for Franklin even as he
approached death. Jesus had established the best system
of morals and religion in the history of the world,
Franklin continued, though Christianity itself had
undergone some corrupting changes since the time of
Jesus. He concluded:

> I have . . . some Doubts as to his Divinity,
> tho' it is a Question I do not dogmatize
> upon, having never studied it, & think it
> needless to busy myself with it now, when
> I expect soon an Opportunity of knowing
> the Truth with less Trouble.[36]

Late in the evening of April 17, 1790, Franklin died
with a picture of the day of judgment by his bedside.
Almost twenty thousand citizens observed his solemn
funeral procession in Philadelphia. At the front of the
cortege marched "the clergymen of the city, all of them,
of every faith."[37] He was buried in the cemetery of
Christ Church. ✤

6. THE RELIGIOUS VIEWS OF GEORGE WASHINGTON

*H*istorians have learned much about George Washington's religious practices and beliefs, not only from his own writings but also from the observations and experiences of persons who knew him. At the start of the twenty-first century, Washington's religious views continue to be the subject of controversy.

Washington was baptized and raised in the Established Church of Virginia. His wife, Martha, was a devoted Anglican and regular churchgoer. By the standards of the eighteenth-century, Washington was religiously active. As an officer prior to the Revolution, he read services for his soldiers when no chaplain was available and required officers and men not on duty to attend. He scrupulously observed the fast days of the Church of England prescribed for the English Army. He served as a vestryman and churchwarden in the Episcopal Church. He is commonly credited with surveying and mapping Virginia's Truro Parish and with persuading its vestry to change the location of Pohick Church, its principal church. From the reports of visitors to Mount Vernon, he occasionally said grace at the table.

During his presidential years, Washington occasionally worshiped in churches of other denominations, but he normally attended Anglican and Episcopal churches. In Virginia his regular churches were Pohick Church in Fairfax County and later Christ Church in Alexandria. In New York City, he attended

St. Paul's Chapel of Trinity Parish and, less frequently, Trinity Church on Wall Street (the church in which James Monroe was married and from which he was buried). When the nation's capital was in Philadelphia, he attended Christ Church (where Franklin also attended) and, less frequently, St. Peter's Church. His diary indicates that he worshiped more frequently during national crises and when he was living in cities. The assistant rector of his church in Philadelphia attested to Washington's "regular attendance."[38]

The interior of St. Peter's Church, Philadelphia, where Founding Fathers often worshiped

The fervor and devoutness of Washington's religion has long been the subject of conflicting assertions. According to the statements of several Revolutionary officers made long after the Revolution, Washington not only was a "constant attendant" at church services but also kept a strict Lord's Day, or Sabbath. But if a contemporaneous source—Washington's diary—is used as an index, he attended church somewhat more than once a month while living at Mount Vernon, and sometimes less. In 1760, the diary indicates that Washington went to church four times during the first five months of the year. In 1768, it records that Washington attended divine services on fifteen Sundays.

True, the conditions of weather and of the roads affected church attendance in rural Virginia. Pohick Church was seven miles from Mount Vernon, and Christ Church was nine miles in a different direction. Moreover, the diary may not include some of Washington's journeys to church on Sunday. Yet the diary also indicates that Washington passed up church on many Sundays, choosing instead to visit relatives and friends, to receive visitors, to go fox-hunting, to travel, or, most frequently, to remain at Mount Vernon "alone all day."

When Washington did attend church, he was by all testimony a reverent worshiper. But in the fashion of the Deists, he seems to have remained indifferent to two significant rites of his church. Like many of the other Founding Fathers who were raised Anglican, he was never confirmed. Confirmation was available after the Episcopal Church secured bishops in the 1780s, and by going forward for confirmation Washington would have provided an example to other Episcopalians. At age eighty-four, for example, James Madison's mother was confirmed when an Episcopal bishop finally visited her rural parish. [39]

Even more significantly, Washington apparently avoided the sacrament of Holy Communion. Writers continue to debate whether Washington received Holy Communion before or during the Revolutionary War, but the convergence of evidence seems to indicate that he did not receive it after the war. And therein lies a story.

During the eighteenth century, the typical Anglican or Episcopal church celebrated the sacrament of the Holy Communion four times a year. On those "Sacrament Sundays," rectors added communion—which all Anglicans were technically supposed to receive at least once a year—to the end of the normal Sunday service of Scripture readings, Psalms (which were sung), prayers, and a sermon. Although the percentage of churchgoers who remained for the communion was low except during Easter, the sacrament represented a principal way in which Anglicans displayed a commitment to Jesus Christ. To receive the bread and wine, a worshiper stood up, walked forward from the pew, and knelt before the holy table. Anglicanism also taught that Christ was present in the elements of the Holy Communion—a belief that Deists would have seen as superstition.

Much of the evidence that Washington remained on such Sundays for the communion service consists of what a judge would term hearsay. That which is not second hand raises questions of credibility.[40] Far more persuasive is the account of Eleanor Parke "Nelly" Custis, Washington's adopted granddaughter, that she and Washington always left church at the end of the regular service on Communion Sundays and then sent the carriage back from Mount Vernon to pick up Martha, who had remained.[41] Also instructive is the testimony of the gentlemanly William White, Washington's bishop and pastor when the seat of government was in Philadelphia. White was simultaneously bishop of Pennsylvania and rector of the three Episcopal churches in Philadelphia. Late in his life, he answered an inquiry about Washington's attendance at communion services with the following discreet words: "...truth requires me to say, that General Washington never received the communion, in the churches of which I am parochial minister. Mrs. Washington was an habitual communicant."[42]

White had the overall charge of the three churches, but he had an assistant at each. The Rev. James Abercrombie, who was in charge of Christ Church, objected so much to the practice of the President of the United States (and others) walking out of church prior to communion that he preached a sermon on public worship. In it he spoke of the "unhappy tendency of . . . those in elevated stations who invariably turned their backs upon the celebration of the Lord's Supper." Although the sermon named no one, Washington correctly assumed that the message was "a very just reproof" directed especially at him. Realizing that he was setting a bad example, he never again attended Christ Church on Sacrament Sundays. This solution was presumably not what the Rev. Mr. Abercrombie had in mind.

Repetitive patterns tell their own story.[43] If these are the actions (or non-actions) of a Deist, what do Washington's private letters and public statements say about his religious views? His public statements contain the majority of his statements about religion. Aides-de-camp and presidential staff wrote much of this material, and historians have noted that the tone of Washington's addresses became more fervent after the appointment of two particular speech writers. But the staff knew Washington's mind. Additionally, since the original manuscripts display changes made in Washington's hand—such as his substitution of "Great Spirit" for "God" in the draft of a formal letter to an Indian tribe—Washington undoubtedly read most of the statements written for him by others before they were issued.

With only a few exceptions (which may or may not have stemmed from the work of assistants), Washington's speeches, orders, official letters, and other public communications on religion give a uniform picture. They seem clearly to display the outlook of a Deist. Their references to religion lack emotion. They omit such words as "God," "Father," "Lord," and "Savior." In their place, they use such deistic descriptive phrases as "the Deity," "the Supreme Being," "the Grand Architect," and "the Great Ruler of Events." They refer infrequently to Christianity and rarely to Jesus Christ.

The most common reference in these official documents is to "Providence." They display Washington's belief that the almost miraculous victory of the colonists as well as the successful creation of the new republic stemmed from the invisible workings of Providence. He seemed to view Providence as the actions of a benevolent, prescient, all-powerful God who created life and guided its development, but who remained somewhat distant and impersonal.

Like Deists, Washington was more concerned with morality and ethics than with adhering to the doctrines of a particular church. He seemed to have no interest in theology. Favoring freedom of conscience for all Christians, Jews, Deists, and freethinkers, he helped establish religious liberty and toleration as central principles in the new American government. He also believed that organized religion played a useful role in society by promoting morality, order, and stability. His replies to the concerns raised by various religious bodies during his presidency—including Jews and Roman Catholics—display his considered reflections on these issues.

Thus he required revolutionary military forces to have chaplains, insisted that his soldiers attend Sunday services, and ordered Thanksgiving services after victories. He talked about death with resignation and stoicism. While on his deathbed—with Martha sitting close by, his personal servant standing near, his physician James Craik starring helplessly into the fire, his other physicians waiting downstairs, and a group of his house servants standing anxiously by the bedroom door—Washington never asked for an Episcopal clergyman. After uttering his last words of "Tis well" and taking his own pulse, he died peacefully on the night of December 14, 1799. Four days later, he was buried after Episcopal and Masonic funeral services. All of this is in keeping with an interpretation of Washington as a Deistic Episcopalian. [44]

The Apotheosis of George Washington *displays his near-deification by Americans upon death*

Yet some writers do not depict Washington as a Deist. Shortly after his death, the religion of the first president became the subject of controversy. Seeking to demonstrate the role that orthodox Christianity played in the founding of the United States, evangelical writers began to portray the Father of His Country as a devout Christian who devoted an impressive amount of time to prayer.

Books such as *The Life of George Washington* by Mason Locke Weems (a book that first appeared in 1800) and Edward C. McGuire's *The Religious Opinions and Character of Washington* (New York, 1836) informed readers of the supposed piety of George Washington. They contained stories of Washington holding Holy Communion services before battles; of a stranger who turned out to be Washington taking lodging in a humble home and spending most of the night in prayer; of Washington visiting small rural churches and inspiring the congregations with his religious fervor; of Washington escaping into the forests during encampments to pray in solitude.

Kept in continuous publication until the 1920s, the biography by "Parson Weems" became one of the best-selling books in American history. As late as the 1890s, in his biography of Washington, Woodrow Wilson passed on Weems's story of a little girl overhearing Washington cry out before a battle: "The Lord God of gods, the Lord God of gods, He knoweth, and Israel he shall know; if it be in rebellion, or if in transgression against the Lord, save us not this day." [45] The closing decades of the twentieth century saw a number of works by evangelical writers reasserting the arguments that

Washington (as well as many of the other Founding Fathers) was in reality an orthodox Christian.[46]

When these pious stories began to appear shortly after Washington's death, many of the general's contemporaries—including Jefferson, Madison, and Bishop White—disputed the depictions. "Sir, he was a Deist," one of Washington's pastors declared in a discussion of the question. Since then, disagreements over Washington's religious beliefs have periodically broken into public print. Early in the twentieth century, letters arguing for and against Washington's belief in the divinity of Christ occupied pages of a leading New York newspaper. Senator Henry Cabot Lodge was among those who argued for Washington's orthodoxy.[47]

In such disputes evangelical and patriotic writers tend to find orthodoxy and zeal in Washington's religion. Professional historians, however, find the chain of evidence supporting the stories of Washington's exemplary piety weak. One author, for example, said that the *Rev. D.D. Field* told *her* that a *Mrs. Watkins told him* that *when she was a girl*, Washington . . . ." Such hearsay evidence (italicized in the quotation) is not valid historical proof. Parson Weems became famous for his story of young George Washington and the cherry tree, which he added to the fifth edition of his biography in 1806. Weems declared that he had heard the story from an old woman who was a cousin of Washington and who had grown up with him. Weems's standing as an historian was low even among his fellow Episcopal clergy in Virginia.

Today most historians believe that the stories of Parson Weems and of other writers who depicted Washington as a pious Christian have no more basis in fact than his story of the cherry tree.[48] Nevertheless, these stories not only elevated Washington to near mythological status but also created legends about him that have refused to die. ✤

7. THE RELIGIOUS VIEWS OF JOHN ADAMS

*I*f Washington's religious views remain a subject of disagreement today, those of John Adams se no such debate. Adams was the first president who was a Unitarian—a faith which, in Adams's case, could be described with some accuracy as "Christian Deism." Since the time of Adams, Unitarianism has broadened in America to include schools of thought that view themselves as neither theistic nor Christian. In the eighteenth and early nineteenth centuries, however, it was a form of supernaturalist Christianity that taught that God was one—a *unit*—and not three—a *tri-unit*. In doing so, Unitarians believed that they had restored the view of the original Christians that Jesus was in some way commissioned or sent by God but that he remained subordinate to him.

At one point in early Christianity, the majority of Christians did not believe in the doctrine of the Trinity. They believed that God was a unipersonality and that Jesus was subordinate to God. Of the two kinds of early anti-Trinitarians, one school held that Jesus was a demigod who had come down from Heaven as a messenger; their rallying cry was "Jesus was from above." The second school held that Jesus was a human whom God had raised to a divine status because of his obedience and morality while on earth; their rallying cry was "Jesus was from below." Adams seems to have fallen into the second category, though he became more rationalistic than many Unitarians.

In the fourth century, Trinitarianism won out in Christianity. Driven from the Roman empire, the anti-Trinitarians gradually disappeared, reviving (though persecuted by Protestants and Roman Catholics alike) in the Reformation period. The rationalizing tendencies of the eighteenth century and its emphasis on morality as the essence of religion increased their appeal. In eastern New England, Unitarianism emerged in the later eighteenth-century in combination with Enlightenment thought. It also grew as a reaction against the revivalistic emotionalism of the Great Awakening. Objecting not only to the doctrine of the Trinity but also to specific Calvinist teachings such as total depravity (the corruption of humanity since the fall of Adam and Eve), Unitarians became the left-wing of the established Congregationalist churches. To orthodox Christians they were heretics, but in their own minds they were restorers of the primitive Christianity that had existed prior to the Trinitarian definitions of the fourth century.

For decades the orthodox Calvinists and the new "rational Christian" or "liberal Christian" Unitarians struggled in New England for control of the denomination and of Harvard College. By the second decade of the nineteenth century, it was clear that the rupture would be permanent. Finally, 125 Congregationalist churches—most located within forty miles of Boston—joined in 1825 to form the American Unitarian Association. Their number included First Parish Church in Quincy, the long-time church of the Adams family. In 1815, Adams stated that in his experience Unitarianism in New England was not a new movement. Rather, he said, it had existed for at least sixty-five years.

Thus, while increasingly holding Unitarian sentiments, Adams was technically a Congregationalist most of his life. Raised in a church-going family in the

Daughter of a Congregationalist minister, Abigail Adams shared her husband's Unitarian faith

established Congregationalist church of Massachusetts and baptized in the parish church in Quincy, he planned at a young age to enter the ministry. While he was at Harvard, however, an acrimonious theological debate between his Enlightenment-influenced pastor at the Quincy church and traditional Calvinists caused Adams to change his views. Siding (as most of the younger parishioners did) with the minister and rejecting the dogmatism and intolerance that seemed to accompany religion, Adams became a schoolmaster and then a lawyer. Retroactively, his parish church dated its adherence to Unitarianism to this controversy of the 1750s.

But religion and church-going remained important to Adams throughout his life. He married Abigail Smith, the daughter of a Congregationalist minister. Describing himself as "a church-going animal," he typically went to church twice on Sundays. He believed in a personal God, in a guiding Providence, and in life after death. He rejected Paine's views of the Bible and Christianity, criticizing him for the antagonism he displayed. As president, he used such distinctly Christian phrases as "Redeemer of the World," "The Great Mediator and Advocate," and "the grace of His Holy Spirit" in his thanksgiving proclamations—phrases which Unitarians of the time (many of whom believed in the miracles recorded in the Bible) could use without contradicting their doctrine of the unipersonality of God.

Additionally, he continued a colonial tradition by twice calling for national fast days to renew the nation's sense of divine mission. Believing it imperative that the world follow the ethical teachings of Jesus, he viewed himself as a Christian. "The Christian religion, as I understand it," he declared to Benjamin Rush in 1810:

> is the brightness of the glory and the express
> portrait of the eternal, self-existent independent,
> benevolent, all-powerful and all-merciful
> Creator, Preserver and Father of the Universe. . . .
> Neither savage nor civilized man without
> a revelation could ever have discovered or
> invented it.[49]

Like other Deists, however, Adams substituted a simpler, less mysterious form of Christianity for the Christianity he had inherited. Reading and reflection caused him to discard such beliefs as the Trinity, the divinity of Christ, total depravity, and predestination (the idea that God had predestined humans to heaven or to hell). God, he declared, "has given us Reason, to find out the Truth, and the real Design and true End of our Existence." Thus he asserted that humans should study nature and use reason to learn about God and his creation.[50]

Above all, Adams opposed religious oppression and narrow-mindedness. "Twenty times, in the course of my late Reading," he wrote to Jefferson in 1817, "have I been upon the point of breaking out, 'This would be the best of all possible Worlds, if there were no Religion in it'." Adams then qualified this "fanatical" comment by declaring that "without Religion this World would be Something not fit to be mentioned in polite Company, I mean Hell." [51]

All of this displays the blend of Unitarian Christianity and rational thought that was the religion of John Adams. Like many of his contemporaries, he brought the religion in which he was raised into the court of reason and common sense and judged it by what he found. His wife, Abigail—who shared Adams's Unitarian views—did the same. "Let the human mind loose," he once wrote in an outburst of Enlightenment passion. "It must be loosed; it will be loose. Superstition and despotism cannot confine it."[52] Adams followed these words with the assertion that Christianity would surely triumph if the human mind were loosed. His statement indicates that he belongs somewhere in the category of Unitarian Christian or Christian Deist. ❖

8. THE RELIGIOUS VIEWS OF THOMAS JEFFERSON

*T*homas Jefferson epitomized what it meant in America to be a man of the Enlightenment. At his estate of Monticello, he displayed busts of Bacon, Locke, and Newton. Incredibly broad in interests and abilities, Jefferson was sufficiently interested in religious matters that one scholar has described him as "the most self-consciously theological of all America's presidents." Religion, the writer declares, "mesmerized him, enraged him, tantalized him, alarmed him, and sometimes inspired him." [53]

Although no record of Jefferson's baptism exists, he was undoubtedly baptized as an infant by a priest of the Church of England. He could remember his mother teaching him prayers from the Book of Common Prayer. His father, Peter Jefferson, a planter and surveyor, served as a vestryman in the local Anglican parish. Educated in the academies of Anglican parsons, young Jefferson spent important years of study under the Rev. James Maury, an Anglican minister and graduate of William and Mary who owned an abundant scholarly library.

At age sixteen, Jefferson entered the College of William and Mary. Of the seven clergy then on its faculty, six were Anglican clergy. But the seventh—a layman, William Small—proved by far the most influential. A product of the Scots Enlightenment, Small taught mathematics, ethics, rhetoric, and belles lettres. He introduced Jefferson to Enlightenment thinkers and sparked a lifelong passion in him for their teachings.

During and after his years at William and Mary, Jefferson copied an enormous amount of the writings of Deistic thinkers into his copy books. By his thirtieth year, he had read and digested most of the principal thinkers of the Enlightenment. Since he could read French, Jefferson became one of the minority of American Deists who was strongly influenced not only by the Scots and English Enlightenment but also by its more radical French counterpart. Among America's Founding Fathers, he became the principal philosophe.

Despite his heterodoxy, Jefferson remained outwardly an Anglican and Episcopalian throughout life. In 1772, an Anglican clergyman presided at his marriage to Martha Skelton Wayles. Although the orthodox and evangelical bishop of Virginia who succeeded Bishop Madison in 1814, Richard Channing Moore, maintained no relationship with him, Jefferson committed the religious care of his children to the Episcopal Church. He also contributed generously to the support of St. Anne's Parish (of which Monticello was a part) and continued to record the births, marriages, and deaths of family members in his father's prayer book.

In Jefferson's time, as today, the Anglican-Episcopal tradition permitted its members a broad channel of belief. To the left and right of that channel, the Book of Common Prayer and the creeds of early Christianity placed buoys to mark the boundaries of Anglican belief. "Here thou may go but no farther," the buoys seemed to say. During his adult life, many Deistic views of Jefferson went well beyond the Anglican buoys on the left. But he never formally departed from his ancestral faith. When he died in 1826, an Episcopal minister presided at his funeral.

Knowing their controversial character, Jefferson was reticent about his religious views. When he sent his thoughts on religion (often in great detail) to friends, he generally requested that they show them to no one. Despite his caution, Jefferson's religious views had become well known in the country as early as 1800, when he ran successfully for the presidency. Jefferson himself was to blame for this exposure, for his one book, *Notes on the State of Virginia* (published in France in 1785 and in England in 1787), contained certain passages that seemed to display him as a Deist.

Thus it was not surprising that Americans generally saw Jefferson's opponent Adams as the believing Christian in the presidential election of 1800. Adams's Federalist ally, Alexander Hamilton, a longtime rival of Jefferson, smeared the Virginia candidate as "an atheist in religion and a fanatic in politics."[54] The Congregationalist ministers of New England, generally Federalists in political loyalty, went so far as to assert that Christians would be forced to hide their Bibles as well as to worship in secret if the "unchristian" Jefferson were elected. In the years since 1800, many writers have analyzed Jefferson's religion. Essentially he seems—like many other Deists—to have been a "restorationist."

The restorationist ideal exists in such areas as politics, constitutional theory, and world religion. In all fields, restorationists attempt to restore a lost set of truths. Christian restorationists believe in a golden era—generally the New Testament period—from which the church has fallen away (or "apostacized"). Protestantism is a form of Christian restorationism, though some of its forms—for example, the Churches of Christ or the Baptists—are more restorationist than others. Whatever their specific programs, the goal of all Christian restorationists is to restore the faith once delivered by Jesus to the saints to its supposed original purity and power.

Deism inevitably tended toward restorationism, in that many of the movement's adherents believed that some combination of external forces had added false doctrines to the original teachings of Jesus. For Ethan Allen, "Craft and Ignorance" had added "excrescences" to Christianity. For Thomas Paine, "Christian Mythologists, calling themselves the Christian Church" had "set up a system of religion very contradictory to the character of the person whose name it bears," a system of "pomp and revenue in pretended imitation" of Jesus's life of "humility and poverty." [55]

After initially fearing that he could no longer believe in the religion in which he was raised, Jefferson read Joseph Priestley's *History of the Corruptions of Christianity* at some point after the Revolution. A one-time Presbyterian minister, a noted scientist (the discoverer of oxygen), and the author of numerous unorthodox tracts on religion, Priestley founded the Unitarian Society in London in 1791. Three years later, he fled England for America after publicly defending the ideals of the French Revolution, a stance with which Jefferson sympathized. Through Priestley's book, Jefferson came to believe that the combined effect of power-hungry monarchs and corrupt "priests" had despoiled the original, pristine teachings of Jesus. But beneath these corruptions—which Jefferson labeled with such words as "nonsense," "dross," "rags," "distortions," and "abracadabra"—Jefferson, like Priestley, came to believe there lay a fulcrum of eternal truth.

Jefferson's view of Jesus displays his restorationism. He regularly read the Bible. But he revered Jesus as a reformer and moral exemplar rather than (as Adams did) a savior. As a result, Jefferson used scissors and razor to excise from his New Testament the corruptions that he believed its writers had placed upon the original teachings of Jesus. Since Jefferson's God was a God of reason, Jefferson removed anything that appeared unreasonable from the gospels.

Such an approach meant, of course, that the Sage of Monticello cut out the prophesies and miracle stories and focused instead on Jesus's ethical teachings and parables. In scholarship, it has always been possible to declare that the Apostle Paul's profoundly influential letters took Christianity in the wrong direction. Choosing that option, Jefferson removed from the New Testament not only Paul's letters but also the letters attributed to Peter, John, and Jude.

Published almost a century after Jefferson's death, his version of the New Testament—titled *The Life and Morals of Jesus* (and other titles)—displays Jefferson's Deistic views of Jesus. In good restorationist fashion, Jefferson believed he had removed the barnacles of corruption from the New Testament. He now believed that the character of Jesus would emerge as "the most innocent" and "the most eloquent . . . that has ever been exhibited to man."[56]

"To the corruptions of Christianity I am, indeed, opposed," he wrote to Benjamin Rush, "but not to the genuine precepts of Jesus himself. I am a Christian in the only sense in which I believe Jesus wished any one to be; sincerely attached to his doctrines, in preference to all others; ascribing to himself every human excellence, and believing he never claimed any other." [57]

Martha "Patsy" Jefferson Randolph, raised by her father in the Anglican tradition

As his derogatory use of the word "priests" indicates (a term he applied not only to medieval Roman Catholic clergy but also to the contemporary Calvinist ministers of New England), Jefferson's Deism made him anti-clerical. Yet where Christianity was concerned, Jefferson was not anti-institutional, for he firmly believed that morality was rooted in religion. He liked to listen not only to good speeches but also to good sermons. Thus he contributed to the building funds of Episcopal, Baptist, and Presbyterian congregations.

Jefferson attended church with some regularity, even inventing a fold-up stool to use when he went to the "union services" conducted by ministers of various denominations at the Albemarle County Courthouse. In the 1780s he helped to raise money to support Charles Clay, an evangelical Anglican rector and supporter of the American Revolution who left St. Anne's Parish (Jefferson's home Episcopal parish) after a disagreement with the vestry over salary. He remained friends for life with the Rev. Mr. Clay, who left the active ministry after the 1780s but apparently remained an orthodox Episcopalian.[58]

That Jefferson attended and supported other churches does not make him a Baptist, Presbyterian, or evangelical Episcopalian. Like many churchgoers, he was always able to tune out points of doctrine with which he disagreed. He remained a Deist in rejecting the rituals and sacraments of institutional religion as the proper forum for worship. For Jefferson, true worship consisted of love and tolerance for human beings according to the ethical teachings of Jesus. He viewed these precepts as "the most pure, benevolent, and sublime which have ever been preached to man." [59] However Christians bickered about the fine points of dogma, he hoped that they and others could agree about the morals of Jesus.

Jefferson also opposed the strong influence that institutional Christianity had on the higher education of his time. When a member of the board of visitors at William and Mary in the 1770s and 1780s, he helped to abolish its divinity school and its two divinity professorships. In their place he substituted professorships in the secular fields of science and law. When he saw that he could not remove the deeply embedded Anglican-Episcopal ethos from William and Mary, he established his own university, the University of Virginia. For some decades, Jefferson's university was essentially a Deistic institution, with neither a religious curriculum nor a chaplain. Its first board of visitors included three American presidents (Madison, Monroe, and Jefferson himself) of Deistic religion. Characterized by religious heterodoxy, its early faculty included the leading Unitarian George Ticknor.

As his religious views developed, Jefferson's understanding of God went beyond that of many Deists. Like many of the Founding Fathers, he believed in a governing and overriding Providence that guided the affairs of the U. S. Like other Deists, he valued intellectual and spiritual freedom and abhorred organized Christianity's tendency toward dogmatism. He believed that no government had the authority to mandate religious conformity, and his Act for Establishing Religious Freedom (1786) helped guarantee the right to freedom of conscience.

Jefferson is often described as a Unitarian. Although he designed the first Episcopal Church in Charlottesville, it is that city's Unitarian church that is named for him. This identification of Jefferson with Unitarianism seems accurate. With the major exception of Bishop Madison, whom he (like Franklin and all of the Virginia Founding Fathers) knew from his work at William and Mary, he distrusted Trinitarian Christian clergy, viewing them as enemies of the simple teachings of Jesus. As Jefferson saw it, rational empirical investigation determined what constituted reality. When viewed from this perspective, the Trinity was "incomprehensible jargon" and "abracadabra." Like other Deists, he viewed mystery as a disguise for absurdity.

For this reason, he refused to serve as godfather for children of friends in Anglican baptisms, for godfathers had to profess a belief in what he viewed as the unreasonable doctrine of the Trinity. "The person who becomes sponsor for a child, according to the ritual of the Church in which I was educated," Jefferson politely wrote to a friend who asked him to serve as a godparent in 1788, "makes a solemn profession before God and the world, of faith in the articles, which I had never sense enough to comprehend, and it has always appeared to me that comprehension must precede assent." [60]

Whether Jefferson would have formally left the church of his ancestors is unclear. But he remains listed in many books as an Episcopalian rather than a Unitarian for the probable reason that Piedmont Virginia contained no Unitarian church. When he lived in Philadelphia, he attended a Unitarian church. And in some famous correspondence with a Unitarian minister, he predicted that Unitarianism would soon sweep the nation:

> I rejoice that in this blessed country of free inquiry and belief, which has surrendered its creed and conscience to neither kings nor priests, the genuine doctrine of only one God is reviving, and I trust there is not a young man now living who will not die an Unitarian.[61]

Like Adams, Jefferson would have fallen into the second category of Unitarians—those who believed that Jesus was "from below." But unlike some early Unitarians, he did not go beyond believing that Jesus became the moral example for humans while he was below. His view of Jesus contained no role for a virgin birth, incarnation, resurrection, miracles, or adoption into divine status.

In his last years, Jefferson clearly moved towards a more traditional interpretation of Christianity. He valued Jesus as a person even more highly. Unlike some Deists, he came to believe in prayer and in a life after death. But belief in an afterlife and in a God who hears prayer were standard Unitarian beliefs of the time. Holding them did not move Jefferson into the category of orthodoxy. His great grandson classified him as a conservative Unitarian.[62] That description may be as good as we can give of a man who classified himself religiously as "of a sect by myself, as far as I know."[63]

Thomas Jefferson's religion was monotheistic, restorationist, reason-centered, Jesus-centered, anti-mystery, anti-medieval, anti-Calvinist, and anti-clerical. A reformer in religion as well as in politics, the founder of a major university he hoped would become a beacon of the Enlightenment, an American who believed he had separated the gold from the dross in government and religion, Jefferson wanted to tear down what he considered false to allow what he considered true to shine through. ✤

9. THE RELIGIOUS VIEWS OF
JAMES MADISON

*B*orn in 1751 in King George County, Virginia, James Madison was baptized by an Anglican parson three weeks after he was born. His father, a small planter, was a vestryman of St. Thomas Parish; his mother was known for her devoutness. Madison received his preliminary schooling in academies run by Anglican clergy. Probably because of its reputation for Christian orthodoxy, the family sent him not to the Deistically-inclined William and Mary but rather to the College of New Jersey, then the principal training ground for American Presbyterian clergy.

After graduating in 1771, Madison remained for a year to study Hebrew and ethics under its president, the Rev. John Witherspoon. A man who combined Presbyterian orthodoxy with an advocacy of the Scottish Common Sense philosophy that gave a decided role to human reason, Witherspoon later became the only clergyman to sign the Declaration of Independence. When Madison left college and returned to the family estate of Montpelier in Orange County, Virginia, he witnessed the persecution and jailing of religious dissenters in adjacent Culpeper County by the Established Church—*his* church. At the age of twenty-two, he came down firmly on the side of religious freedom, arguing that only liberty of conscience could guarantee civil and political liberty. As the years went on, he increasingly became convinced that the separation of church and state was best not only for the state but also for the churches.

Madison fought for religious liberty throughout his political career. When Virginia adopted a new constitution in 1776, he insisted that the document guarantee freedom of conscience rather than mere toleration. In 1785 he wrote the anonymous and influential *Memorial and Remonstrance against Religious Assessments,* which helped defeat a bill in the Virginia House of Delegates calling for state subsidies to religious bodies. He also devoted energy to ensuring the adoption of Thomas Jefferson's Act for Establishing Religious Freedom and worked to have its principle enumerated in the federal Bill of Rights.

Despite Madison's activity on behalf of religious freedom, historians know relatively little about his private views on religion. Any investigator who wishes to get beyond Madison's reticence must look not only at what he did and did not do, but also at what he said and did not say in the area of religion.

In his formal education, Madison experienced both Anglican and Presbyterian interpretations of Christianity. Like Adams, he considered a career in the ministry while in college. By the time he left the College of New Jersey, he was able to read the Bible in both Hebrew and Greek, though he apparently did not continue to study it. When he returned home to Montpelier, he conducted family worship, a mark then (as now) of orthodoxy.

During his presidency, Madison held the President's Pew at St. John's Episcopal Church, adjacent to the White House. He married a Quaker, Dolley Payne, who not only attended Episcopal services with him but also presented herself for confirmation as an Episcopalian after his death. Though he rarely wrote or spoke publicly about religious subjects once he embarked on his legal career, he maintained a lifelong interest in religion. When Jefferson asked him for a list of books on theology for the library of the new University of Virginia (whose cornerstone Monroe laid), Madison responded with a list that showed a wide familiarity with theological literature. The evidence seems clear that he remained respectful of institutional religion throughout his life.

Unlike his wife and mother, however, Madison never went through the rite of confirmation. As president he opposed executive proclamations that used religious language. When circumstances forced him to issue one (such as during the War of 1812), he kept the language as neutral and non-sectarian as possible. His belief that citizens should voluntarily support religion led him to oppose the appointment of chaplains for Congress and for the army and navy.

At a White House dinner in 1815, he purposely seated the Boston gentleman-scholar George Ticknor by himself and Dolley Madison. A co-founder of the Boston Public Library and a leading Unitarian layman, Ticknor reported the contents of the conversation:

> He talked of religious sects and parties,
> and was curious to know how the cause of
> liberal Christianity stood with us, and if
> the Athanasian creed was well received by
> our Episcopalians. He pretty distinctly

intimated to me his [high] regard for
Unitarian principles. . . . Mr. M. gave
amusing stories of early religious persecu-
tions in Virginia, and Mrs. M. entered
into a defence and panegyric of the
Quakers, to whose sect, you know, she
once belonged.[64]

Defining the interrelationship of the Trinity, the
Athanasian Creed was written in the fourth and fifth centuries. Like other Anglicans, Madison grew up reciting it
during church services, in words such as the following:

. . . we worship one God in Trinity, and
Trinity and Unity; Neither confounding
the Persons: nor dividing the Substance
. . . . as also there are not three incompre-
hensibles uncreated, nor three uncreated:
but one uncreated, and one incomprehensible . . . . the Father is made of none: neither created, nor begotten. The Son is of
the Father alone: not made, nor created,
but begotten. The Holy Ghost is of the
Father and of the Son: neither made, nor
created, nor begotten, but proceeding. . . .
He therefore that will be saved: must thus
think of the trinity. our Lord Jesus Christ,
the Son of God, is God and Man . . .
One altogether; not by confusion of
Substance: but by unity of Person . . . .
this is the Catholick Faith: which except a

man believe faithfully, he can not
be saved.

Dropped from the American Book of Common Prayer by the Protestant Episcopal Church in 1785, the Athanasian Creed was the kind of highly technical document that caused Enlightenment figures to turn towards Deism or Unitarianism. It was precisely the kind of document critics viewed as containing "the incompressible jargon of the Trinitarian arithmetic."[65]

If this pattern seems to indicate Deism, so do the comments and experience of Madison's contemporaries. One of the longest statements comes from the patrician William Meade, the third Episcopal bishop of Virginia, who knew not only the Madisons but also the Episcopal clergy who ministered to the family. Seeking in later years to answer persistent inquiries about Madison's "religious sentiments," Meade wrote down what he remembered:

> During his stay at Princeton a great revival
> took place, and it was believed that he
> partook of its spirit. On his return home
> he conducted family worship in his
> father's house. He soon after offered for
> the Legislature, and . . . his opponents
> [objected] that he was better suited to the
> pulpit than to the legislative hall. His reli-
> gious feeling, however, seems to have been
> short-lived. His political associations with
> those of infidel principles, of whom there

In his old age James Madison may have returned to Christian orthodoxy

were many in his day, if they did not actually change his creed, yet subjected him to
the general suspicion of it.

Whatever may have been the private
sentiments of Mr. Madison on the subject
of religion, he was never known to declare
any hostility to it. He always treated it
with respect, attended public worship in
his neighbourhood, invited ministers of
religion to his house, [and] had family
prayers on such occasions, though he did
not kneel himself at prayers. Episcopal
ministers often went there to see his aged
and pious mother and administer the
Holy Communion to her.

Eleven years before Madison died, an Episcopal
cleric asked the former president about his views of
God. The minister reported that the former president
answered in a way that concealed his beliefs. On one
visit to Montpelier, Meade reported that he and
Madison held their one and only discussion about religion. "The conversation took such a turn," the bishop
wrote, "as to call forth some expressions and arguments
which left the impression on my mind that his creed
was not strictly regulated by the Bible."

But having indicated that Madison was a Deist,
Meade concludes his review of the fourth President's
religion with surprising words:

At his death, some years after this, his
minister, the Rev. Mr. [William] Jones,
and some of his neighbours openly
expressed their conviction, that, from his
conversation and bearing during the latter
years of his life, he must be considered as
receiving the Christian system to be
divine.[66]

Bishop Meade held a tough-minded view of other
people's religion. If he is correct that James Madison
returned to a more traditional view of Christianity, that
is unsurprising. Old age is often the time when people
return "home" by embracing the faith in which they
were raised. Thus Madison may have become an orthodox Christian in his beliefs in his final years, though
readers should note that Bishop Meade also tries to
make a case for the Christian orthodoxy of George
Washington. Except for Meade's account, however, the
pattern of Madison's religious associations and the comments of contemporaries clearly categorize the fourth
president of the United States as a moderate Deist. ✤

10. THE RELIGIOUS VIEWS OF JAMES MONROE

*J*ames Monroe was born on April 28, 1758, in a home four miles from the birthplace of George Washington. He was the eldest son of Spence Monroe, a small planter in Westmoreland County. Born into an Anglican family, Monroe was baptized in Washington Parish. He studied at Campbelltown Academy, a noted academy run by the Rev. Archibald Campbell, the rector of Washington Parish; John Marshall was a classmate. In 1774, he went to an Anglican college, William and Mary, where the president and faculty were clergy of the Established Church. There Monroe was required to attend not only daily morning and evening prayer in the College chapel but also Sunday worship at near-by Bruton Parish Church.

As political tension with Great Britain mounted, Monroe became active in the revolutionary cause and later served as an officer in the Continental Army. In 1780 Monroe left the army as a colonel to study law at William and Mary and later in Richmond under Thomas Jefferson, who became a lifelong friend and political mentor. In the next decades, Monroe practiced law in Fredericksburg and served in the Virginia House of Delegates and on the Council of the State of Virginia. He gained additional political experience in the Congress, as a Minister to France, Great Britain, and Spain, and as secretary of state and secretary of war during the War of 1812. In 1816, Monroe was elected fifth president of the United States. His two terms as president are noted for the Era of Good Feelings, the Missouri Compromise, the establishment of the Indian Territory, the purchase of Florida, and especially the Monroe Doctrine.

In 1786, at age twenty-eight, Monroe met and married the seventeen-year-old Episcopalian Elizabeth Kortright of New York City. Their marriage occurred at her home parish church, Trinity Church on Wall Street. The couple raised their two daughters, Eliza and Maria Hester, as Episcopalians. Thirteen years later, Monroe built and moved to the plantation of Highland, adjacent to Jefferson's estate of Monticello in Albemarle County, Virginia. After serving two terms and leaving the presidency at the age of sixty-seven, Monroe gave up his dream of retiring to Highland. Selling it to satisfy creditors, he settled on his plantation of Oak Hill in Loudoun County, Virginia, which was closer to the nation's capital.

Elizabeth Monroe, whose increasingly fragile health had provided another reason for moving closer to the District of Columbia, died on September 23, 1830. Ten months later, on July 4, 1831, Monroe died in New York City at the home of his younger daughter, Maria Hester Gouverneur. He was the third American president— Jefferson and John Adams were the other two—to die on July 4.

Monroe's funeral occurred at Trinity Church, where the church's rector and the Episcopal bishop of New York conducted the service from the Book of Common Prayer. In the same month, the Episcopal bishop of Virginia conducted a memorial service for Monroe in his native state. In 1858 his coffin was disinterred from its burial vault in a private cemetery in Manhattan and moved to the Episcopal Church of the Annunciation on West 14th Street in Manhattan, where the public could view it. The coffin was then moved by steamer to Richmond and reinterred with pageantry in Hollywood Cemetery. A Presbyterian minister delivered the prayer of commitment.

During his lifetime, Monroe lived in six Virginia parishes—Washington (where he was born), Bruton (where he went to college), Henrico (where he studied law and served as governor), St. George's (where he practiced law), St. Anne's (when he lived at Highland), and Shelburne (when he retired to Oak Hill). He also served on the board of visitors of William and Mary, where Episcopal membership was almost a prerequisite for service. While president, he occupied the President's Pew in St. John's Episcopal Church opposite the White House; its rector officiated when Maria Hester was married at the White House in 1820. Yet Monroe's biographers have rarely mentioned his religious views. Even those who have written books on the religion of the American presidents have found little to say when they have reached the religion of the fifth president of the United States.

The family papers of James Monroe are missing, as are the papers of his daughters. Tench Ringgold, a friend of Monroe during his later years, reported that Monroe burned his correspondence with his wife after her death. These family letters are the most likely places where Monroe would have discussed religious matters. While a substantial number of private letters of Monroe have survived, as have his public papers and writings, they contain remarkably little about religion.

One letter written during the American Revolution to Peter S. Duponceau does contain clear religious sentiments. A native of France, Duponceau served as military secretary to Frederick Wilhelm Augustus von Steuben, the Prussian-born inspector general of the Continental Army. During the winter of 1778, he and Monroe (who were close in age) became good friends. Receiving word that Duponceau had become seriously ill, Monroe wrote to him from Valley Forge in April, 1778:

> From what the Baron has informed us, much heightened by your melancholy letter, I am induced to believe that declining nature scarce supports human existence. Your turn of mind I observe. . . is well adapted to the gradual decay of life. . . . tis the summit of christian fortitude and heroism to prevail over the views of this transitory life, and turn the mind on the more lasting happiness of that to come.
>
> The blessed influence of heaven is, I hope, on you: beware of heresy: danger, ruin, and perpetual misery await it. But while life remains, it is necessary you should have some thing more than mere repentence [sic] to amuse your thoughts on.

Monroe then declared that he was sending Duponceau (who had been raised Roman Catholic) some books by two Anglican authors. "The moral of the one," he concludes, "[was] so correspondence [correspondent?] with the scripture of the other that you will esteem it a well calculated discourse on virtue and religion."[67]

The letter was the work of a nineteen-year-old who had been through three battles and had narrowly escaped death at the Battle of Trenton. It may display a certain amount of rote piety, for Monroe had a strong background of religious instruction and knew the language of orthodox Christian belief. Nevertheless, the letter spoke of "christian fortitude and heroism," mentioned heaven, warned against "heresy," and indicated that its writer is sending several books "on virtue and religion" written by Anglican clergy.

To draw too many conclusions from a single letter written by a young man in the midst of war is unwise. But the letter does permit speculation that Monroe's view of Christianity may have changed at some point between the Revolution and his emergence into public service. For in later years Monroe's public statements and speeches were remarkably silent about religious matters. Neither his public utterances nor his writings—including his autobiography—cite the Bible, nor did they make references to Jesus Christ. In his first inaugural address, Monroe praised the concept of religious freedom, boasting that Americans may worship "the Divine Author" in any manner they choose. This same address declared that "the favor of a gracious Providence" has guided the

United States. It concludes with Monroe declaring that he enters the presidential office with "fervent prayers to the Almighty that He will be graciously pleased to continue to us that protection which he has already so conspicuously displayed in our favor."

Monroe's second inaugural address spoke of his "firm reliance on the protection of Almighty God." When his speeches referred to the Deity, he used only the stock Deistic phrases. No more than half of the numerous short speeches he made while on his tour of the nation in 1817 contained religious references. Instead, Monroe talked about civic virtues.

Though many of Monroe's published letters deal with political issues, they did make passing references to personal matters. Discussion of religion, however, was absent. Even the surviving personal correspondence of Monroe avoids religious issues. In Monroe's time, gentlemen customarily wrote letters of advice to children, including godchildren and children of friends. When they wrote to sons in college, for example, fathers might urge them to attend religious services. In one such letter, Jefferson began by advising his nephew Peter Carr on books to read but then changed to advising him about Scriptural interpretation and theological claims.[68]

Nothing of the sort appears in Monroe's extant letters of advice. When he wrote detailed letters advising his nieces and nephews how they could live happy and productive lives, he included no comments about spiritual matters. When James Monroe, Jr.—the son of Monroe's brother, Joseph Jones Monroe—became unruly while a cadet at West Point, Monroe sent him a detailed letter full of advice. But the letter mentions neither God nor religion. Even though Monroe had many connections in New York, he did not counsel his nephew, as was customary in such letters, to see any noted ministers or to attend certain churches. When his only son, James Spence Monroe, died at the age of sixteen months in 1800, Monroe was clearly overwhelmed. The funeral service and burial were at St. John's Episcopal Church, Richmond, where the family worshiped while Monroe was governor. But the letters Monroe wrote to others about the death include no references to the consolation of religion. When Elizabeth died in 1830, Monroe wrote to a number of their friends saying how devastating her death was, but he failed to mention any religious beliefs that may have proved comforting. In contrast, when John Adams and Jefferson exchanged letters upon the death of Abigail Adams, both spoke of the consolations of a future state where they would meet loved ones again.[69]

James and Elizabeth Monroe did own a substantial collection of art that included religious subjects. Documented by inventories, their collection included a Madonna and Child, a head of John the Baptist, a painting of the Virgin Mary, and a painting of Mary Magdalene. But the inclusion of religious art was typical in a collection of that time and says little about religious belief. Monroe's selection of art parallels that of Jefferson and of other Virginia and English contemporaries. A typical Protestant gentleman's home might have paintings of religious subjects by continental Roman Catholic artists, mixed with landscapes, old masters, contemporary art, engravings and prints, and classical sculpture. In addition, the evidence indicates that Elizabeth Kortright Monroe, who was especially interested in art and architecture, was instrumental in the collecting.

Monroe's known library included three copies of the Bible. Fewer than a dozen books in the library (some of which are plainly presentation copies) were theological or biblical. He knew Bishop James Madison—second cousin of President Madison—from their years together at William and Mary. But when Madison became the first Episcopal bishop of Virginia in 1790 and Episcopalians could participate in the rite of confirmation for the first time, Monroe did not seek to be confirmed. Though he does not seem to have been anticlerical (as Jefferson was), he appears neither to have corresponded with Bishop Madison nor to have initiated correspondence with other clergy.

During his decades at his Albemarle estate of Highland, Monroe may have attended Forge Church, a deteriorating colonial structure within easy riding distance from his estate. The Episcopal bishops never allude to him in their reports of visitations to the church, however, nor does Bishop William Meade include the Monroes in his list of families who supported the Episcopal Church in Albemarle County.[70] Jefferson never reported being accompanied by his neighbor Monroe when he attended services at the Albemarle County courthouse in Charlottesville.

On his three-month national good-will tour in 1817, Monroe visited ten states, going as far west as Ohio. Throughout New England as well as in

Pittsburgh, his visits to towns and cities included clergy in receptions and in ceremonial processions. On some Sundays Monroe went to church—usually to Episcopal services, but sometimes to those of other denominations.

The record is unclear as to how many Sundays Monroe attended church on the tour, but one service stands out because of his reaction. On June 22, 1817, accompanied by Horace Holley (a leading Unitarian minister in Boston), Monroe attended the Congregational meeting house in New Haven pastored by the Rev. Nathaniel Taylor. A stern defender of Calvinism, Taylor and his "New Haven Theology" married conservative Calvinism with the evangelical currents of the Second Great Awakening. The sermon may have included not only the hard marrow of traditional Calvinism but also the critiques of Unitarianism and the Episcopal Church for which Taylor was also known. A record of the service declares that "Mr. Monroe was taken by surprise by a sermon from Rev. Dr. Taylor, an extreme Calvinist, much to the chagrin of the Rev. Horace Holl[e]y, a high Unitarian."[71]

Religion was not a primary concern of Monroe. When he died, he left no deathbed statement. Instead, historians have only the assertion of a friend that he died resigned to his fate. The eulogies by his contemporaries at his funeral commemorations in New York, Richmond, and Boston speak of Monroe in terms of patriotism and statesmanship; none even mentions his religious faith. Following Monroe's death, writers did not circulate pious literature about his religious beliefs, as they did about Washington.

Also significant are the reminiscences of Bishop Meade, who knew the Virginia Founding Fathers and their families well. When Meade discusses their religion in his two-volume *Old Ministers, Churches and Families of Virginia*, he devotes considerable space to Washington. Additionally, he gives detailed information on the religious beliefs of Madison and dismisses Jefferson's views as "disbelief." But in five mentions of Monroe—who had served with the bishop's father in the Revolution—he says nothing about religion. Similarly, Monroe's biographers rarely introduce the subject. "When it comes to Monroe's . . . thoughts on religion," one such writer declares, "less is known than that of any other President."[72]

But one known item about Monroe may shed additional light on his religious beliefs: he was a Freemason. The ties between Deism and Freemasonry were close. Freemasonry claims ancient origins, but probably originated in England in the twelfth century as a religious society that guarded the secrets of the craft of masons. Over the centuries it developed into a secret international fraternity concerned with the moral and religious improvement of its members. From England it spread to France, Germany, Italy, and other countries.

The movement took on a new character in the eighteenth century. In Roman Catholic countries, the Masonic lodges tended to form an underground movement antagonistic not only towards Roman Catholicism but also towards organized religion in general. Hence from the eighteenth century until recent years, Popes prohibited Roman Catholics from joining the Masons.

In Protestant countries, Freemasonry tended to require a belief in a monotheistic God from its members and to advocate an undogmatic religion that claimed to represent the essence of all religions. Wherever Masonry went, its rituals used drama and allegory to emphasize its message but gave a preeminent place neither to the Bible nor to Jesus. A Muslim, Jew, or Christian—or anyone who could accept its statements about a divine being—could belong. When the Founding Fathers use such terms as "the Grand Architect" to speak of God, they are using language that comes directly from Freemasonry and not from the Bible.

A fraternal organization that provided a club for men at a time when clubbing represented a principal form of entertainment, Masonic lodges appeared in the American colonies early in the eighteenth century. Like Deistic belief, its lodges grew in popularity in the decades following the Revolution, and Deistic views were widespread in them. Masonic membership was common among leading figures in the Revolution. Franklin and Lafayette were both Masons. Washington not only took his oath of office on a Masonic Bible but also laid the cornerstone of the U. S. Capitol using a Masonic trowel. Monroe became a Mason in 1775 while a student at William and Mary, joined the lodge in Fredericksburg while practicing law, and remained at least somewhat involved in the Masons throughout his life. During his second term as president, he was made an honorary member of the Washington Naval Lodge No. 4.[73]

As his Episcopal marriage, wedding, and funeral

indicate, James Monroe maintained a life-long affiliation with the church in which he was raised. The Episcopal Church ministered to the Monroe family and claimed them as its own. Yet the surviving evidence indicates that Monroe was not a Christian in the traditional sense. Neither his private nor his public writings indicate that he ever experienced a sense of the mystery or awe that is at the heart of orthodox Christianity. No evidence exists to show that he was an active or emotionally-engaged Christian. How the Anglican interpretation of Christianity influenced his character and personality, and what depths of religious feelings he may have experienced while attending worship, scholars may never know.

Like Washington, Monroe was neither a philosophical nor a highly intellectual man. He was most effective when he solved problems and worked on practical matters. Unlike Franklin, Adams, Jefferson, and Madison, he did not seem to spend extensive time considering why the universe was so. These personality traits may explain the lack of information about his spiritual side.[74]

In sum, Monroe seems to have been an Episcopalian of Deistic tendencies who valued civic virtues above religious doctrine. No one cared more for the identity of the new nation. In his adult years, his passion always seems to have been directed towards the cause of the United States. From his eighteenth to his seventy-third year, he was almost continually in public service. "He had found [the nation] built of brick," John Quincy Adams declared in his eulogy of Monroe, "and left her constructed of marble."[75] Reflective, tactful, practical, simple in his tastes, democratic in his convictions, Deistic in his religion, James Monroe may have been the most skeptical of the early American presidents. ❖

11. THE PAST IS A FOREIGN COUNTRY

*W*hat, then, is definitely known about the religion of the Founding Fathers of the American republic?

Three months after Monroe's death, Bird Wilson, a professor at the General Theological Seminary in New York City—the oldest theological seminary in the Episcopal Church—preached a sermon purporting to answer that question. His credentials for providing the answer were excellent. Wilson's father, James, was himself a Founding Father. One of George Washington's original appointments to the U. S. Supreme Court, James Wilson had been a member of the Continental Congress and a signer of the Declaration of Independence. In the Constitutional Convention of 1787, his influence had probably ranked second only to that of James Madison.

A conservative in politics, James Wilson had been a communicant of Christ Church, Philadelphia, and an intimate friend of Bishop White. White was, in fact, the godfather of Bird Wilson. When White retired, he wanted Bird Wilson to succeed him as Bishop of Pennsylvania—a position Wilson missed securing only by one vote. Wilson later became White's first biographer.

Born in 1777, Bird Wilson was raised in the city most associated with the American Revolution and with the founding of the new republic. He grew up in close contact with the leading personalities of the new republic. He was twenty-three years old when the national capital moved from Philadelphia to the District of Columbia. One can easily imagine the visitors to his father's home in Philadelphia and the conversations he must have overheard or participated in while growing up.

Additionally, Wilson had a distinguished career as a lawyer and jurist in Philadelphia before being ordained to the Episcopal ministry by his godfather. If anyone in 1831 knew the difference between appearance and reality in the religious beliefs of the Founding Fathers, it would have been Bird Wilson.

In his sermon delivered in October of that year, Wilson attacked the current stories that were circulating about the admirable religious piety of the Founding Fathers. Washington, he said in the sermon, had not been an orthodox Christian; in reality he had really been a typical eighteenth-century Deist. Wilson cited support on this point from clergy who had known Washington. Then he went on to state that "among all our presidents downward, *not one* was a professor of religion, at least not of more than Unitarianism."[76]

In the more than 170 years since James Monroe's death and Bird Wilson's sermon, writers have continued to examine the religious faith of the Founding Fathers. They have tended to place the Founders' religion into one of three categories—non-Christian Deism, Christian Deism, or orthodox Christianity. The vast majority of American historians attached to colleges or universities have placed them in one of the first two categories.

But in recent decades evangelical writers, many of whom are pastors, have decried a secular bias among academic historians. Downplaying the influences of Deism on the Founding Fathers, they have argued that the Founders genuinely adhered to Christian belief.

While the Founders "certainly valued human reason," one evangelical writer recently asserted, "they followed the Scottish Common Sense philosophers in believing that rational thought did not contradict Christian doctrine. The Trinity and the resurrection, therefore, appealed even to rationalists like Jefferson, Adams, and Madison." [77]

The six Founding Fathers surveyed in this study appear to have been neither wholehearted Deists nor orthodox Christians. They maintained their formal affiliations with Christian denominations, though none who were Anglican seem to have become full church members. In the spirit of the times, they questioned doctrines that they believed could not be reconciled with human reason. As a result, they rejected such Christian teachings as the Trinity, the virgin birth, the resurrection, and the divinity of Jesus. Yet all of these six Founders believed in a guiding Providence and—with the possible exception of Monroe—in a life after death. These affirmations separated them from the radical Deists of their time.

The Founders respected the ethical teachings of Jesus. They believed that simple virtue and morality were of far greater importance than adherence to a particular set of religious doctrines. Above all, they valued freedom of conscience and despised religious tyranny and dogmatism. By enacting laws to protect religious freedom, they ensured that Americans would maintain the right to worship this Creator in any manner they chose.

That the Founding Fathers adopted many Deistic patterns of thought is unsurprising. It would have been far more surprising if they had become evangelical Protestants, Roman Catholics, Russian Orthodox, Scandinavian Lutherans, or Orthodox Jews. In the formative years of their lives, Deism was a prevailing religious sentiment not only in parts of the United States but also in France and in other European countries. In Virginia it was the dominant interpretation of religion among educated males. To a greater or lesser extent, all of these six Founding Fathers accepted and "expressed the characteristic ideas and prepossessions of [their] century—its aversion to 'superstition' and 'enthusiasm' and mystery:

> its dislike of dim perspectives; its . . . clarifying
> scepticism; its passion for freedom and
> its humane sympathies; its preoccupation
> with the world that is evident to the senses;
> [and] its profound faith in common sense,
> in the efficacy of reason for the solution of
> human problems and the advancement of
> human welfare." [78]

The Founding Fathers of the United States were remarkable, even noble men. Like most people, they understood their religion in the terms of their background and of their day. Those trained in parsons' academies had studied the Bible more thoroughly than all but a small percentage of Christians have today. In the spirit of their times, they appeared less devout than they were—which seems a reversal from modern politics.

Today many Americans are concerned that their presidents be sincere men and women of faith. These

NOTES

1. Alexis de Tocqueville, *Democracy in America* (New York, 1994), 308.

2. John Adams, *Diary and Autobiography*, eds. L.H. Butterfield, et al., *The Adams Papers*, 4 vols. (Cambridge, MA, 1961), II:150. See also David McCullough, *John Adams* (New York, 2001), 84.

3. John Adams, et al., *Adams Family Correspondence*, eds. L.H. Butterfield, et al., *The Adams Papers*, 6 vols. (Cambridge, MA, 1963), I:167. See also McCullough, 84.

4. Quoted in Edwin Scott Gaustad, *A Religious History of America*, new rev. ed. (San Francisco, 1990), 70.

5. Non-predestinarian theologians take such claims seriously, but try to reconcile Biblical teachings on predestination with the concept that humans are free to accept or to reject salvation. Calvin and other predestinarians cited such episodes and passages as the calling of Abraham, the selection of Israel as the Chosen People, the selection of Jacob over Esau and similar Divine selections, and such New Testament passages as Matthew 20:23, Romans 8:28-30, Ephesians 1:3-14, II Timothy 1:9, and the ninth through eleventh chapter of Romans.

6. The text even of traditional hymns can change over the years. All quotations in this study are taken from *The Hymnal 1982* (New York, 1985), the official hymnal of the Episcopal Church.

7. More than ten American colleges claim colonial founding. But in all cases these claims stem from an institution's decision that a parson's school or classical academy in their area—what Americans would today call a primary or secondary school—was the direct ancestor of their college. In the twentieth century, as colleges adopted new institutional ancestors, some changed their founding date several times. Thus one four-year college now lists its date of

founding as 1696, though a history of the college published in 1890 "by the Alumni Association" is titled *1789-1889. Commemoration of the One Hundredth Anniversary of* (the college's name follows). On this subject the overriding question has to be: did a college exist at this place in the year claimed? Uniformly applied, this criterion would change the dates of founding of some of the ten colonial colleges named in this study, for many started their first students at a pre-college level to prepare them for study at a level intended to equal that of Oxford and Cambridge or Calvin's Genevan Academy. But all ten institutions would still have genuine founding dates in the colonial period.

8. Edwin S. Gaustad, *Sworn on the Altar of God: A Religious Biography of Thomas Jefferson* (Grand Rapids, Mich, 1995), 164. Adams' list includes three kinds of Unitatiarians.

9. Winthrop S. Hudson and John Corrigan, *Religion in America,* 5th ed. (New York, 1992), 30.

10. Maryland Toleration Act of 1649 at http://www.mdarchives. state.md.us/msa/speccol/sc2200/sc2221/000025/html/title page.html.

11. Maryland Toleration Act of 1649.

12. Edward C. Papenfuse, Jr. *Two Acts of Toleration: 1649 and 1826* (Annapolis, Md, 1999) at http://www.mdarchives. state.md.us/msa/spelcol/sc2200/sc2221/000025/html/intr o.htm.

13. Hugh F. Lefler, ed., *North Carolina History Told by Contemporaries* (Chapel Hill, 1934), 56.

14. *Colonial Records of North Carolina,* ed. William L. Saunders, 10 vols. (Raleigh, 1887), I: 601-602.

15. "The Spiritual Travels of Nathan Cole," *William and Mary Quarterly*, XXXIII, no. 1 (1976): 2-3, paragraphing added.

16. This discussion of George Whitefield's oratorical ability is found in Chapter 8 of Benjamin Franklin's autobiography. Paragraphing has been added.

17. Walter Isaacson, *Benjamin Franklin: An American Life.* (New York, 2003), 110.

18. The quotation is from Paul Johnson, *A History of the American People* (New York, 1997), 109.

19. Daniel Preston, ed. *The Papers of James Monroe: A Documentary History of the Presidential Tours of James Monroe* (Westport, CT, 2002), I: 123.

20. Moncure C. Conway, ed., *The Writings of Thomas Paine* 4 vols. (New York, 1894-96), IV: 322.

21. L. W. Gibson, "Deism," in A. A. Benson, ed., *The Church Cyclopedia* (Philadelphia, 1883), 224, italics added.

22. Quoted in Robert T. Handy, *A Christian America* (New York, 1984), 15-16.

23. Thomas Paine, *The Age of Reason*, ed. Philip S. Foner (Secaucus, NJ, 1974), 55, 162-163.

24. Thomas Paine, *The Age of Reason*, 68.

25. Gaustad, *Sworn on the Altar,* 34-41. The descriptions come from Anthony Ashley Cooper, Third Earl of Shaftesbury and Elihu Palmer.

26. The poet was Philip Freneau (1752-1832). For the poem, see http://www.americanpoems.com/poets/philipfreneau/onthe.shtml.

27. Paine, *The Age of Reason*, 50.

28. The quotation can be found in Part I of Paine's *The Rights of Man.* See, for instance, Philip S. Foner, ed., *The Complete Writings of Thomas Paine*, 2 vols. (New York, 1945), I: 293.

29. Denis Diderot. The phrase appears in his posthumous "Dithyramb on the Festival of Kings."

30. William Meade, *Old Churches, Ministers and Families of Virginia*, 2 vols. (Baltimore, 1966), I: 175.

31. Meade, *Old Churches*, II: 99.

32. Isaacson, 19.

33. A. Owen Aldridge, "The Alleged Puritanism of Benjamin Franklin" in ed. J.A. Leo Lemay, *Reappraising Benjamin Franklin: A Bicentennial Perspective* (Newark, Del, 1993), 370.

34. Benjamin Franklin, "On the Providence of God in the Government of the World," eds. Leonard W. Labaree, *et al.* *The Papers of Benjamin Franklin* (New Haven: 1959-), I: 264.

35. Leonard W. Labaree, *et al*, eds., *The Papers of Benjamin Franklin,* 36 vols. (New Haven, 1959--), IX: 121.

36. Franklin B. Dexter, ed., *The Literary Diary of Ezra Stiles,* 3 vols. (New York, 1901), III: 387.

37. Isaacson, 470.

38. James Abercrombie, quoted in Paul Boller, *George Washington and Religion* (Dallas, 1963), 18.

39. Meade, *Old Churches*, II: 92.

40. See, for example, Meade, *Old Churches*, II: 490-492. Similar examples are scattered throughout Meade's two volumes.

41. Nelly Custis (Mrs. Eleanor Parke Custis Lewis) lived for twenty years with her adoptive parents at Mount Vernon. In 1833, at the request of the first editor of Washington's papers—Jared Sparks—she wrote down her memories of Washington's religious practices. Sparks reprinted her letter in his edition of the *Writings of George Washington*, 12 vols. (Boston, 1834-37), XII: 406.

42. William White to Hugh Mercer, 15 August 1835, in Bird Wilson, *Memoir of . . . the Rt. Rev. William White* (Philadelphia, 1839), 197.

43. James Abercrombie to Origen Bacheler, 29 November 1831, in *Magazine of American History*, XIII, (June 1885), 597. See also Boller, *George Washington*, 33-34. The phrase about "repetitive patterns" comes from C. P. Snow, *In Their Wisdom* (New York, 1974), 144.

44. David L. Holmes, ed. *A Nation Mourns: Bishop James Madison's Memorial Eulogy on the Death of George Washington* (Mount Vernon, Va, 1999).

45. Woodrow Wilson, *George Washington* (New York, 1896), 227.

46. See such works as Peter Marshall, *The Light and the Glory*; Tim La Haye, *Faith of Our Founding Fathers*; William Federer, *God and Country*; Verna Hall, *The Christian History of the American Revolution*; Ben Hart, *Faith and Freedom*; and the various publications of the Providence Foundation of Charlottesville, Virginia. Evangelical leaders such as Pat Robertson and Jerry Falwell also preach and publish on the subject.

47. New York *Herald Tribune*, 26 May 1902.

48. For a thorough analysis of the reliability of the stories of Weems and other early writers on Washington's religion, see Boller, *George Washington*, 3-44.

49. John Adams to Benjamin Rush, 21 January 1810, in *The Microform Edition of the Adams Papers*, 608 reels (Boston, 1954-1959), reel 118.

50. Adams, *Diary*, I: 42-44.

51. John Adams to Thomas Jefferson, 19 April 1817, in *The Microform Edition of the Adams Papers*, reel 123.

52. John Adams to John Quincy Adams, 15 November 1816, in *The Microform Edition of the Adams Papers*, reel 123.

53. Gaustad, *Sworn on the Altar*, xiii-xiv.

54. Gaustad, *Sworn on the Altar*, 92.

55. Paine, *The Age of Reason*, 55, 66.

56. Thomas Jefferson, "Jesus, Socrates, and Others—Letter to Dr. Joseph Priestley, April 9, 1803," in *The Library of America: Jefferson: Writings*, ed. Merrill D. Peterson (New York: 1984), 1120.

57. Thomas Jefferson to Benjamin Rush, 21 April 1803, in *The Writings of Thomas Jefferson*, ed. Albert E. Bergh, 20 vols. (Washington, DC, 1907), X: 379-380.

58. Meade, *Old Churches*, II: 48-51, 61.

59. Thomas Jefferson to Jared Sparks, 4 November 1820, in *Thomas Jefferson: A Chronology of His Thoughts,* ed. Jerry Holmes (New York, 2002), 285.

60. Thomas Jefferson to Justin Pierre Plumard Derieux, 25 July 1788, in *The Papers of Thomas Jefferson,* ed. Julian P. Boyd, *et al.*, 30 vols. (Princeton, NJ, 1950-), 13: 418.

61. Thomas Jefferson to Benjamin Waterhouse, 26 June 1822, in *The Writings of Thomas Jefferson,* XIII: 350.

62. Thomas Jefferson Coolidge, "Jefferson in His Family," in *The Writings of Thomas Jefferson,* XV: iv.

63. Thomas Jefferson to Ezra Stiles Ely, 25 June 1819, in Dickinson W. Adams, ed., *Jefferson's Extracts from the Gospels* (Princeton, 1983), 386-387.

64. George Ticknor, *Life, Letters, and Journals of George Ticknor,* ed. George Stillman Hillard, 2 vols. (Boston, 1909), I: 29-30.

65. Gaustad, *Sworn on the Altar,* 139.

66. Meade's information about Madison's religious faith is found in his *Old Churches,* II: 99-100.

67. James Monroe to Peter Duponceau, 11 April 1778, in Duponceau Papers, J. R. Tyson Transcripts, Historical Society of Pennsylvania. The original of this letter has disappeared. Only the transcript made in earlier decades by a researcher remains.

68. Thomas Jefferson to Peter Carr, 10 August 1787, in *The Writings of Thomas Jefferson,* ed. Paul Leicester Ford, 10 vols. (New York, 1892-99), IV: 429-432.

69. A convenient source for the correspondence between Jefferson and Adams upon Abigail's death is James B. Peabody, ed., *John Adams: A Biography in His Own Words* (New York, 1973), 404-405.

70. Meade, *Old Churches,* II: 50-52.

71. Daniel Preston, ed., *The Papers of James Monroe: A Documentary History of the Presidential Tours of James Monroe* (Westport, CT, 2002), I: 123.

72. Bliss Isely, *The Presidents: Men of Faith* (Boston, 1953), 38.

73. I am indebted to David Voelkel, curator/assistant director of the James Monroe Museum in Fredericksburg, Virginia, for this information.

74. I am indebted for many observations about Monroe and his correspondence to Daniel Preston, editor of *The Papers of James Monroe* at Mary Washington College.

75. John Quincy Adams, *The Lives of James Madison and James Monroe* (Buffalo, 1850), 293-295.

76. Bird Wilson, Untitled Sermon Reported in the Albany (N.Y.) Daily Advertiser on 29 October 1831. See also Boller, *George Washington*, 14-17.

77. To see the variety of arguments about Washington's religion, readers need only search the web for the words "Founding Fathers religion" or "George Washington religion." The quotation comes from an interview in the summer of 2000 with Mark Beliles of the Providence Foundation.

78. This rich description is found in "Benjamin Franklin," *Concise Dictionary of American Biography* (New York, 1964), 312. Later editions of the work continue to us it.

79. L. P. Hartley, *The Go-Between* (New York, 1997), prologue.

ILLUSTRATIONS

1. **Touro Synagogue, Newport, R.I.**
   Courtesy of Touro Synagogue.

2. **Ephrata Solitary Sister in Habit**
   From Julius Friedrich Sachse, *The German Sectaries of Pennsylvania: 1742-1800* (Philadelphia, 1900).

3. **First Baptist Church, Providence, R.I.**
   From Peter T. Mallary, *New England Churches & Meetinghouses: 1680-1830* (New York, 1985).

4. **Yale College and Chapel**
   From Reuben A. Holden, *Yale: A Pictoral History* (New Haven, 1967).

5. **Charles Calvert, Third Lord Baltimore and Second Proprietor of Maryland, by Sir Godfrey Kneller**
   Courtesy of Enoch Pratt Free Library, Baltimore, MD.

6. **George Whitefield**
   From Mark A. Noll, *A History of Christianity in the United States and Canada* (Grand Rapids, MI, 1992).

7. **Francis Asbury**
   From Elmer T. Clark, ed., *The Journal and Letters of Francis Asbury: Volume I* (London, 1958).

8. **Bishop James Madison**
   Courtesy of Virginia Historical Society, Richmond, VA.

9. **Trinity Church, New York City**
   From Leicester C. Lewis, *A History of the Parish of Trinity Church in the City of New York: Part I* (New York, 1898).

10. **John Adams's Copy of Thomas Paine's *Common Sense***
    From James Bishop Peabody, ed., *John Adams: A Biography in His Own Words* (New York, 1973).

11. **Benjamin Franklin**
    From Thomas Fleming, ed., *Benjamin Franklin:*
    A Biography in His Own Words (New York, 1972).

12. **Interior of St. Peter's Church, Philadelphia**
    Courtesy of Cornwall Collection, Archives of the
    Episcopal Church, U.S.A.

13. *The Apotheosis of George Washington*
    Courtesy of Mount Vernon Ladies' Association,
    Gift of Mr. Stanley Deforest Scott.

14. **Abigail Adams at Age 22**
    Courtesy of Massachusetts Historical Society, Boston,
    MA/Bridgeman Art Library.

15. **Martha "Patsy" Jefferson Randolph**
    Courtesy of Monticello/Thomas Jefferson Foundation.
    Portait by Thomas Sully.

16. **James Madison, Circa 1830, by Asher B. Durand**
    Courtesy of The Century Association, New York City.

SELECT BIBLIOGRAPHY BY TOPICS

General Works—Religion, the Revolution, and the Founding Fathers

Albanese, Catherine L. *Sons of the Fathers: The Civil Religion of the American Revolution.* Philadelphia: Temple Univ. Press, 1976.

Bonomi, Patricia U. *Under the Cope of Heaven: Religion, Society, and Politics in Colonial America.* New York: Oxford Univ. Press, 1986.

Butler, Jon. *Religion in Colonial America.* New York: Oxford Univ. Press, 2000.

Cousins, Norman. *The Republic of Reason: The Personal Philosophies of the Founding Fathers.* San Francisco: Harper & Row, 1988.

Gaustad, Edwin S. *Faith of Our Fathers: Religion and the New Nation.* San Francisco: Harper & Row, 1987.

_____. *Neither King nor Prelate: Religion and the New Nation, 1776-1826.* Revised and corrected ed. Grand Rapids, Mich.: Wm. B. Eerdmans, 1993.

Heimert, Alan. *Religion and the American Mind, from the Great Awakening to the Revolution.* Cambridge: Harvard Univ. Press, 1966.

Hutson, James H. *Forgotten Features of the Founding: The Recovery of Religious Themes in the Early American Republic.* Lanham, Md.: Lexington Books, 2003.

_____. *Religion and the New Republic: Faith in the Founding of America.* Lanham, Md.: Rowman & Littlefield, 2000.

Lambert, Frank. *The Founding Fathers and the Place of Religion in America.* Princeton: Princeton Univ. Press, 2003.

Mapp, Alf J. *The Faiths of Our Fathers: What America's Founders Really Believed.* Lanham, Md.: Rowman & Littlefield, 2003.

Miller, William Lee. *The First Liberty: America's Foundation in Religious Freedom.* Expanded and updated ed. Washington: Georgetown Univ. Press, 2003.

Sheldon, Garrett Ward, and Daniel L. Dreisbach. *Religion and Political Culture in Jefferson's Virginia.* Lanham, Md.: Rowman & Littlefield, 2000.

The Religion of the Enlightenment: Deism

Aldridge, Alfred Owen. *Man of Reason: The Life of Thomas Paine.* Philadelphia: Lippincott, 1959.

Davidson, Edward H., and William J. Scheick. *Paine, Scripture, and Authority: The Age of Reason as Religious and Political Idea.* Bethlehem, Pa.: Lehigh Univ. Press, 1994.

Foner, Eric. *Tom Paine and Revolutionary America.* New York: Oxford Univ. Press, 1976.

Fruchtman, Jack. *Thomas Paine and the Religion of Nature.* Baltimore: Johns Hopkins Univ. Press, 1993.

Grean, Stanley. *Shaftesbury's Philosophy of Religion and Ethics: A Study in Enthusiasm.* Athens: Ohio Univ. Press, 1967.

Marshall, John. *John Locke: Resistance, Religion, and Responsibility.* Cambridge: Cambridge Univ. Press, 1994.

Morais, Herbert M. *Deism in Eighteenth Century America.* New York: Columbia Univ. Press, 1934.

Nuovo, Victor. *John Locke: Writings on Religion.* New York: Oxford Univ. Press, 2002.

Kaminski, John P. *Citizen Paine: Thomas Paine's Thoughts on Man, Government, Society, and Religion.* Lanham, Md.: Rowman & Littlefield, 2002.

Pollock, John Charles. *Shaftesbury: The Poor Man's Earl.* London: Hodder and Stoughton, 1985.

Sell, Alan P. F. *John Locke and the Eighteenth-Century Divines.* Cardiff: Univ. of Wales Press, 1997.

Voitle, Robert. *The Third Earl of Shaftesbury, 1671-1713.* Baton Rouge: Louisiana State Univ. Press, 1984.

Walters, Kerry S. *The American Deists: Voices of Reason and Dissent in the Early Republic.* Lawrence: Univ. Press of Kansas, 1992.

_____. *Rational Infidels: The American Deists.* Durango, Colo.: Longwood Academic, 1992.

Wolterstorff, Nicholas. *John Locke and the Ethics of Belief.* Cambridge: Cambridge Univ. Press, 1996.

Benjamin Franklin

Aldridge, Alfred Owen. *Benjamin Franklin and Nature's God.* Durham, N.C.: Duke Univ. Press, 1967.

Anderson, Douglas. *The Radical Enlightenment of Benjamin Franklin.* Baltimore: Johns Hopkins Univ. Press, 1997.

Isaacson, Walter. *Benjamin Franklin and the Invention of America: An American Life.* New York: Simon & Schuster, 2003.

Morgan, Edmund Sears. *Benjamin Franklin.* New Haven: Yale Univ. Press, 2002.

Walters, Kerry S. *Benjamin Franklin and His Gods.* Urbana: Univ. of Illinois Press, 1999.

Wright, Esmond. *Franklin of Philadelphia.* Cambridge: Belknap Press of Harvard Univ. Press, 1986.

George Washington

Alden, John Richard. *George Washington: A Biography.* Baton Rouge: Louisiana State Univ. Press, 1984.

Boller, Paul F. *George Washington & Religion.* Dallas: Southern Methodist Univ. Press, 1963.

Brookhiser, Richard. *Founding Father: Rediscovering George Washington.* New York: Free Press, 1996.

Ferling, John E. *The First of Men: A Life of George Washington.* Knoxville: Univ. of Tennessee Press, 1988.

Flexner, James Thomas. *Washington, The Indispensable Man.* Boston: Little, Brown and Co., 1974.

Longmore, Paul K. *The Invention of George Washington.* Berkeley: Univ. of California Press, 1988.

John Adams

Chinard, Gilbert. *Honest John Adams.* Boston: Little, Brown and Co., 1933.

Ellis, Joseph J. *Passionate Sage: The Character and Legacy of John Adams.* New York: Norton, 1993.

Ferling, John E. *John Adams: A Life.* Knoxville: Univ. of Tennessee Press, 1992.

McCullough, David G. *John Adams.* New York: Simon & Schuster, 2001.

Shaw, Peter. *The Character of John Adams.* Chapel Hill: Published for the Institute of Early American History and Culture, Williamsburg Va., by the Univ. of North Carolina Press, 1976.

Thomas Jefferson

Burstein, Andrew. *The Inner Jefferson: Portrait of a Grieving Optimist.* Charlottesville: Univ. Press of Virginia, 1995.

Cunningham, Noble E. *In Pursuit of Reason: The Life of Thomas Jefferson.* Baton Rouge: Louisiana State Univ. Press, 1987.

Ellis, Joseph J. *American Sphinx: The Character of Thomas Jefferson.* New York: Knopf, 1997.

Gaustad, Edwin S. *Sworn on the Altar of God: A Religious Biography of Thomas Jefferson.* Grand Rapids, Mich: Wm. B. Eerdmans, 1996.

Peterson, Merrill D. *Thomas Jefferson and the New Nation: A Biography.* New York: Oxford Univ. Press, 1970.

Sanford, Charles B. *The Religious Life of Thomas Jefferson.* Charlottesville: Univ. Press of Virginia, 1984.

James Madison

Alley, Robert S. *James Madison on Religious Liberty.* Buffalo: Prometheus Books, 1985.

Banning, Lance. *The Sacred Fire of Liberty: James Madison and the Founding of the Federal Republic.* Ithaca: Cornell Univ. Press, 1995.

Ketcham, Ralph Louis. *James Madison: A Biography.* New York: Macmillan, 1971.

McCoy, Drew R. *The Last of the Fathers: James Madison and the Republican Legacy.* New York: Cambridge Univ. Press, 1989.

Miller, William Lee. *The Business of May Next: James Madison and the Founding.* Charlottesville: Univ. Press of Virginia, 1992.

Rakove, Jack N., and Oscar Handlin. *James Madison and the Creation of the American Republic.* Glenview, Ill.: Scott Foresman and Little Brown, 1990.

James Monroe

Ammon, Harry. *James Monroe: The Quest for National Identity.* Charlottesville: Univ. Press of Virginia, 1990.

Cresson, W. P. *James Monroe.* Hamden, Conn.: Archon Books, 1971.

Cunningham, Noble E., Jr. *The Presidency of James Monroe.* Lawrence: Univ. of Kansas Press, 1996.

Morgan, George. *The Life of James Monroe,* by George Morgan. New York: AMS, 1969.

Preston, Daniel. *A Narrative of the Life of James Monroe with a Chronology.* Charlottesville and Fredericksburg, Va.: Ash Lawn-Highland and the James Monroe Museum and Memorial Library, 2001.

Preston, Daniel, and Marlena C. DeLong, eds. *The Papers of James Monroe: A Documentary History of the Presidential Tours of James Monroe, 1817, 1818, 1819.* Vol. 1. Westport, Conn.: Greenwood Press, 2003.

INDEX

Numbers in *italics* are chapter numbers.
Numbers in **boldface** indicate illustrations.

Franklin, Benjamin, *Chapter 5*; and 2, 5, 16, 28, 44, 45, 48, 51, 56, 60, 67, 71, 73, 80, 104, 125, 126

Franklin, Sarah, 76

Fredericksburg, Virginia, 113, 117, 125

Freneau, Philip, 63

Freemasonry, 68, 85, 124-125

G

General Theological Seminary, New York City, 128

Georgia, colony of, 12, 38-39, 41, 44, 52

Gouverneur, Maria Hester Monroe, 116, 117

Great Awakening, 46-48, 77, 91, 123

H

Hamilton, Alexander, 98

Hampden-Sydney College, 36

Harvard College, 25, 69, 70, 91, 93

Hay, Eliza Monroe, 116

Henry, Patrick, 54

Herbert, Edward (Lord Herbert of Cherbury), 65

Highland (home of James Monroe), 116, 117, 122

Holley, Horace, 123

Holy Communion services, 9, 67, 82-83, 87, 113. See also Lord's Supper.

Huguenots. See Reformed Churches, French.

Huss, John, 11

I

Indians (American). See Native Americans.

J

Jefferson, Martha Skelton Wayles, 97

Jefferson, Peter, 96

Jefferson, Thomas, *Chapter 8*; and 3-5, 48, 50, 51, 54, 56, 60, 63, 69, 70, 71, 88, 94, 108, 109, 115, 116, 120, 121, 122, 124, 126, 130; Thomas Jefferson Memorial Church, Charlottesville, Virginia, 104

Jesuits (Society of Jesus), 32, 34

Jesus of Nazareth, views of Founding Fathers of: as ethical teacher, 77-78, 90, 93, 100-103, 105, 130; divinity of, 76, 78, 90, 94, 105, 110, 114, 130; resurrection from the grave, 76, 105, 130; virgin birth of, 105, 130

David L. Holmes is Professor of Religion
at the College of William and Mary.
A church historian, he is the author of
A Brief History of the Episcopal Church
and other books and articles.